The San Francisco Earthquake: The History of California's

By Charles River Editors

Arnold Genthe's photo of Sacramento St. with fire off in the distance

About Charles River Editors

Charles River Editors provides superior editing and original writing services across the digital publishing industry, with the expertise to create digital content for publishers across a vast range of subject matter. In addition to providing original digital content for third party publishers, we also republish civilization's greatest literary works, bringing them to new generations of readers via ebooks.

Sign up here to receive updates about free books as we publish them, and visit Our Kindle Author Page to browse today's free promotions and our most recently published Kindle titles.

Introduction

Picture of the ruins after the earthquake and fires

The San Francisco Earthquake of 1906

"[I]t does not seem to have affected any one with a sense of final destruction, with any foreboding of irreparable disaster. Every one is talking of it this afternoon, and no one is in the least degree dismayed. I have talked and listened in two clubs, watched people in cars and in the street, and one man is glad that Chinatown will be cleared out for good; another's chief solicitude is for Millet's 'Man with the Hoe.' 'They'll cut it out of the frame,' he says, a little anxiously. 'Sure.' But there is no doubt anywhere that San Francisco can be rebuilt, larger, better, and soon. Just as there would be none at all if all this New York that has so obsessed me with its limitless bigness was itself a blazing ruin. I believe these people would more than half like the situation." – H.G. Wells

On April 18, 1906, most of the residents of the city of San Francisco were sound asleep when the ground started to shake around 5:15 a.m., but what started as fairly soft tremors turned into a violent shaking in all directions. The roar of the earthquake unquestionably woke up residents, at least those fortunate enough not to be immediately swallowed by the cracks opening up in the ground. The earthquake lasted about a minute, but it had enough destructive force to divert the course of entire rivers and level much of the 9th largest city in America at the time.

Unfortunately for San Franciscans, the worst was yet to come. During the earthquake, the city's gas mains and water mains were ruptured, which had the effects of starting a number of fires and preventing the residents from being equipped to fight them. Without water to truly fight the blaze, the city's officials actually resorted to demolishing buildings in hopes of containing the fire, and witnesses reported seeing San Franciscans trapped in the burning buildings being shot by authorities instead of letting them burn alive. The fires lasted three days, and by the time they were done, 80% of the city was in ruins, about 60% of the residents were homeless, and an estimated 3,000-6,000 were dead. In fact, the fires were so devastating that contemporary San Franciscans called the disaster "The Fire."

Although the resulting fires may have done the most damage, the widespread destruction made clear to city leaders that the new buildings would need better safety codes and protection against subsequent earthquakes. The city reinforced new buildings against earthquakes and fixed older surviving buildings to better deal with future earthquakes, and the city also created the Auxiliary Water Supply System to prevent a repeat of the 1906 disaster.

At the same time, there was a determined sense of resolve to rebuild San Francisco into a bigger and better city, and financial assistance flowed to the shattered city from all across the country. Even as refugee camps were set up in parks and sheltered people for a few years, the U.S. Army and other volunteers helped provide for the people, and despite suffering damage amounting to the equivalent of over $6 billion in today's dollars, California governor George C. Pardee was right when he predicted, "This is not the first time that San Francisco has been destroyed by fire, I have not the slightest doubt that the City by the Golden Gate will be speedily rebuilt, and will, almost before we know it, resume her former great activity."

The San Francisco Earthquake and Fire of 1906 & the 1989 Bay Area Earthquake: The History of California's Two Deadliest Earthquakes chronicles the deadliest natural disaster in California's history and one of the most important seismic events on record. Along with pictures of important people, places, and events, you will learn about the San Francisco Earthquake of 1906 like never before.

Damage done in San Francisco's Marina District

The Loma Prieta Earthquake (October 17, 1989)

"I'll tell you what—we're having an earth—" - Al Michaels broadcasting the World Series on ABC as the earthquake struck

"Well folks, that's the greatest open in the history of television, bar none!" – Al Michaels after the ABC feed was restored

On October 17, 1989, millions of Americans tuning in to watch the Oakland Athletics face the San Francisco Giants in the World Series watched the cameras suddenly start to shake violently for several seconds. The national broadcast had just caught an earthquake registering a 6.9 on the Richter scale striking the Bay Area, and by the time the earthquake and the resulting fires were over and dealt with, over 60 people were dead, making it San Francisco's deadliest earthquake since the 1906 earthquake and fire.

The damage and devastation across the Bay Area was widespread, despite the precautions and changes that the region had made in the wake of the 1906 calamity. After that disaster, San Francisco began the process of reinforcing new buildings and seismic retrofitting of old ones to help structures brace for earthquakes, but even in the 1980s they were still more concerned about potential fires resulting from an earthquake. Furthermore, after the earthquake in 1906, San Francisco created an Auxiliary Water Supply System that could distribute water to any section of the city, and the city built it with stringent codes in the event of an earthquake. In fact, just a few years before 1989, San Francisco created a Portable Water Supply System and upgraded the fire departments.

San Francisco's water supply systems worked perfectly, quickly allowing firefighters to put out a fire in the Marina District before it spread, but this time the biggest problem was "liquefaction," in which saturated soil literally melted away as it was unable to hold any more liquid. The shaking of the earthquake then created cracks in the liquefied soil, and attempts to protect buildings from the violent movements could not safeguard them from the land melting away from under it. The most noteworthy damage occurred to several sections of highways in the Bay Area that did not hold up during the earthquake, despite the fact the earthquake in 1906 was much more powerful. A section of the Bay Bridge collapsed, and the double-decker I-880 collapsed at the Cypress Street Viaduct, killing more than 40 people in Oakland.

As with the earthquake in 1906, the 1989 earthquake brought about changes in an effort to make the region safer. One immediate reaction by Bay Area leaders was to do away with double-decker highways; while highways like the Bay Bridge were seismically reinforced and retrofitted, I-880 was demolished, as was I-280 and the Central Freeway. Over the next several years, the Bay Area rebuilt and rerouted these highways, which cost billions of dollars. The unfinished double-decker Embarcadero Freeway, which had been approved over 30 years before the earthquake despite stiff resistance, was also demolished.

The San Francisco Earthquake and Fire of 1906 & the 1989 Bay Area Earthquake: The History of California's Two Deadliest Earthquakes

About Charles River Editors

Introduction

The San Francisco Earthquake and Fire of 1906

    Chapter 1: San Francisco Before the Quake

    Chapter 2: The Earthquake

    Chapter 3: Help

    Chapter 4: Fire

    Chapter 5: Water

    Chapter 6: Dynamite

    Chapter 7: Martial Law

    Chapter 8: Burning Bigotry

    Chapter 9: Rising from the Ashes

    Bibliography

The 1989 Bay Area Earthquake

    Chapter 1: Mother Nature Plays Ball

    Chapter 2: A Blow to San Francisco

    Chapter 3: Pitching In and Helping Out

    Chapter 4: Protection

    Chapter 5: The Fires

    Chapter 6: The Bay Bridge

    Chapter 7: Surviving the Aftermath

    Bibliography

The San Francisco Earthquake and Fire of 1906

Chapter 1: San Francisco Before the Quake

"Jesus left the temple and was walking away when his disciples came up to him to call his attention to its buildings. 'Do you see all these things?' he asked. 'Truly I tell you, not one stone here will be left on another; everyone will be thrown down...There will be famines and earthquakes in various places...For in the days before the flood, people were eating and drinking, marrying and giving in marriage, up to the day Noah entered the ark; and they knew nothing about what would happen until the flood came and took them all away." - Matthew 24:1-2

Whenever a natural disaster strikes, people often assume that there was no way to see it coming, but while that is sometimes the case, there is usually evidence that something bad is about to happen. Such was the case with the earthquake that struck San Francisco on April 18, 1906. Nearly six weeks before it struck, Professor Alexander McAdie recorded a small earthquake in San Francisco, and such small quakes were sometimes precursors to larger problems. However, McAdie also realized that small earthquakes could often be one-time events that didn't signify anything else coming, and San Francisco's location near the San Andreas fault line ensured the city was used to small rumblings. In essence, if McAdie correctly predicted that a bigger earthquake was coming, he would be a hero, but if not, he would find himself a laughingstock. That left him in a conundrum.

Meanwhile, San Francisco had other problems on its mind. It had been a relatively small town until the California gold rush just 60 years earlier, but with people heading west hoping to strike it rich, the city had grown by leaps and bounds. Its population continued swelling with more men looking for gold, more women coming with their husbands, and more businesses looking for customers. Unlike more settled parts of the country that had grown up slowly around entrenched families, San Francisco was a boom town, but at about 60 years old, it had also begun to show its age. Those in charge had their hands full trying to keep the city healthy and looking good, which required a constant influx of services and workers, but by 1906, conflicts between the two had led to unionization and labor unrest. On April 17, the day before the earthquake, Waiters Union threatened to go out on strike.

Then there was the issue of the railroads. San Francisco depended on America's iron arteries to bring in supplies and ship out goods, but railroad companies were also well aware of their importance and happily used it to get what they wanted, including the use of streetcars above ground instead of an underground subway. As the city's leaders considered the proposals before them, more rumors swarmed about bribes and threats being used to buy influence. San Francisco's mayor, "Handsome Gene" Schmitz, was popular among the union leaders and in 1901 became the first member of the recently-formed Union Labor Party to be elected mayor of an American city. However, in 1906, he found himself under scrutiny and accused by many of graft and taking bribes, and not long after the disaster, he would be indicted and convicted on 27 counts of political corruption. His conviction would later be overturned before he served any jail time.

Schmitz

Problems with the railroad were soon overshadowed by issues related to the city's water supply. The day before the earthquake struck, Mayor Schmitz was mulling what to do about the city's plans to divert the nearby Toulumne River so that its water could be used by the citizens of the city. Water in California had always been an issue, especially since the state was quickly becoming more populated that her supplies could support. Of course, there were competing interests for the water, and the President of the nearby Modesto Irrigation District was displeased about the prospect of losing some of his own share of the river that he wrote a complaint to the mayor that was received on April 17.

As the sun went down on April 17, most San Franciscans retired to their homes or to the opera house, where the famous Italian tenor Enrico Caruso was performing. The city fathers were proud to host such a famous singer and looked at it as evidence that their town was growing up and developing a level of culture that might someday rival the cities back east. Caruso himself was pleased with his performance and his reception, later writing, "I was stopping at the [Palace] Hotel, where many of my fellow-artists were staying, and very comfortable it was. I had a room on the fifth floor, and on Tuesday evening, the night before the great catastrophe, I went to bed feeling very contented. I had sung in "Carmen" that night, and the opera had one with fine éclat. We were all pleased, and, as I said before, I went to bed that night feeling happy and contented."

An illustration of the Palace Hotel (which was destroyed during the disaster)

Others were literally "marrying and giving in marriage." Dr. George Blumer later wrote, "On the evening of April 17th 1906…I acted as best man at the wedding of my old friend Doctor August Jerome Lartigan to Doctor Kate Brady. It was a church wedding and was followed by a beautiful supper at the home of the bride's parents out in the Mission. I did not get to bed until about 1:30 a.m. on the morning of April 18th."

Many people, especially those living near the warehouse district, were awakened suddenly by sirens wailing, but it wasn't due to the earthquake. Instead, it was a three alarm fire at the Central California Canneries located at the corner of Bay and Mason Streets. The fire broke out sometime before 11:00 p.m. and was already in fully fury when the fire department was called. By the time the last flame was doused and the firemen were able to return to their houses, it was nearly 5:00 in the morning. Barely taking time to strip off their soot-stained clothes and wash their faces, they collapsed into their beds and fell quickly into a sound sleep. The ensuing 20 minute nap was the last real rest any of them would get for days.

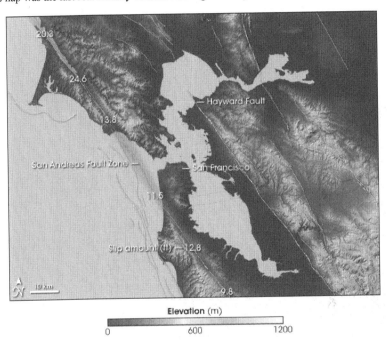

The San Andreas fault zone and its proximity to San Francisco

Caruso

Chapter 2: The Earthquake

"I had $600.00 in gold under my pillow. I awoke as I was thrown out of bed. Attempting to walk, the floor shook so that I fell. I grabbed my clothing and rushed down into the office, where dozens were already congregated. Suddenly the lights went out, and every one rushed for the door. Outside I witnessed a sight I never want to see again. It was dawn and light. I looked up. The air was filled with falling stones. People around me were crushed to death on all sides. All around the huge buildings were shaking and waving. Every moment there were reports like 100 cannons going off at one time. Then streams of fire would shoot out, and other reports followed. I asked a man standing next to me what happened. Before he could answer a thousand bricks fell on him and he was killed. A woman threw her arms around my neck. I pushed her away and fled. All around me buildings were rocking and flames shooting. As I ran people on all sides were crying, praying and calling for help. I thought the end of the world had come." – G.A. Raymond

For most people, the San Francisco Earthquake of 1906 came as a rude awakening, literally. When the quake began on April 18 at 5:15 in the morning, most people were still sound asleep in their beds. Arnold Genthe had been at the opera house the night before and recalled, "After a quiet supper party with some friends, I walked home and went to bed with the music of Carmen still singing in my ears. It seemed as if I had scarcely been asleep when I was awakened by a terrifying sound–the Chinese porcelains that I had been collecting in the last years had crashed to the floor…The whole house was creaking and shaking, the chandelier was swinging like a pendulum, and I felt as if I were on a ship tossed about by a rough sea. 'This can't go on much longer,' I said to myself. 'When a house shakes like this, the ceiling is bound to collapse. As soon as the plaster begins to fall, I'll cover my head and accept what comes.'"

Peter Bacigalupi had a similar experience: "On the morning of the 18th of April I was awakened from a sound slumber by a terrific trembling, which acted in the same manner as would a bucking bronco. I sat up in bed with a start. My bed was going up and down in all four directions at once, while all about me I heard screams, wails, and crashing of breaking china-ware and nick-nacks. I was very quietly watching the clock on the mantel, which was doing a fancy stunt, while the ornaments in the parlor could be heard crashing to the floor. A great portion of plaster right over the head of my bed fell all around me, and caused a cloud of dust, which was very hard to breathe through."

A toppled statue 30 miles away from San Francisco on the Stanford University campus

Of course, not everyone was asleep. Thomas Chase was on his way to work and thus had the unique experience of seeing the effects of the earthquake in action on the streets: "I heard a low distant rumble. It was coming from the west. Louder and louder. I stopped and listened. Then it hit. Power and trolley lines snapped like threads. The ends of the power lines dropped to the pavement not 10 feet from where I stood, writhing and hissing like reptiles. Brick and glass showered about me. Buildings along First Street from Howard to Market crumbled like card houses. One was brick. Not a soul escaped. Clouds of that obliterated the scene of destruction. The dust hung low over the rubble in the street."

Picture of the damage on Howard St.

The SS *Columbia* lying up against a dry dock

Another eyewitness who was already awake at the time described similar experiences: "Of a sudden we had found ourselves staggering and reeling. It was as if the earth was slipping gently from under our feet. Then came the sickening swaying of the earth that threw us flat upon our faces. We struggled in the street. We could not get on our feet. Then it seemed as though my head were split with the roar that crashed into my ears. Big buildings were crumbling as one might crush a biscuit in one's hand. Ahead of me a great cornice crushed a man as if he were a maggot - a laborer in overalls on his way to the Union Iron Works with a dinner pail on his arm."

One of the men on the streets, G.A. Raymond, explained how he escaped to safety on Market St.: "I met a Catholic priest, and he said: 'We must get to the ferry.' He knew the way, and we rushed down Market Street. Men, women and children were crawling from the debris. Hundreds were rushing down the street and every minute people were felled by debris. At places the streets had cracked and opened. Chasms extended in all directions. I saw a drove of cattle, wild with fright, rushing up Market Street. I crouched beside a swaying building. As they came nearer they disappeared, seeming to drop out into the earth. When the last had gone I went nearer and found they had indeed been precipitated into the earth, a wide fissure having swallowed them. I was crazy with fear and the horrible sights. How I reached the ferry I cannot say. It was bedlam, pandemonium and hell rolled into one. There must have been 10,000 people trying to get on that boat. Men and women fought like wildcats to push their way aboard. Clothes were torn from the backs of men and women and children indiscriminately. Women fainted, and there was no water at hand with which to revive them. Men lost their reason at those awful moments. One big, strong man, beat his head against one of the iron pillars on the dock, and cried out in a loud voice: 'This fire must be put out! The city must be saved!' It was awful."

Among the more than 1,000 people who lost their lives that day, hundreds died instantly when their homes collapsed around them. For instance, many of the poorest citizens of the city lived in the South-of-Market tenements, and those poorly made apartments collapsed under their feet before they even had time to get out of bed or understand what was happening. Some of them were likely lucky enough to die instantly, but many remained injured and trapped for hours before passing away. The most fortunate residents managed to dig their way out of the rubble, often with the help of firemen or the neighbors.

As with many similar disasters, many of those who were killed were firefighters, and the first one injured was not trying to save others. In fact, Fire Chief Engineer Dennis T. Sullivan was asleep in the fire house when he suffered a mortal injury. In a terse, official report, Battalion Chief Walter Cook described what happened: "On the 18th inst. at 5:13 a.m. our quarters were carried down by the dome of the California Hotel…The roof and third and second floor came down through the apparatus floor to the cellar. Apparatus floor resting on coal pile; Third floor occupied by the late Chief and his wife…When the crash ceased we started at once to dig for the Chief and Mrs. Sullivan…. While so digging the Chief walked from the rear of the pile. P. Gallagher and Jerry Collins, Chief's Operator, assisted him into the St. George Stables. Chief's Operator, drove him away at once to the Hospital. Mrs. Sullivan was taken out shortly afterwards and we carried her into the California Hotel where a Doctor took charge of her." At first, it seemed that Sullivan was not seriously injured, but he had been badly burned when he landed next to a broken radiator and died a few days later. Upon Sullivan's death, John Dougherty suddenly became the Acting Chief, just in time for the biggest crisis to ever hit the city.

Another fireman, James O'Neill, was also killed before he ever got to fight the famous blaze. He was watering the horses outside his station when the quake hit, and when the American Hotel collapsed next door, one of the walls fell onto the fire station and O'Neill himself. Officer Max

Fenner, a cop walking his beat, was also killed by a falling wall that morning. According to Police Captain Thomas Duke, Fenner "was standing opposite the Essex Lodging House, a seven-story brick building on Mason near Ellis Street, when the earthquake occurred. He observed that the front wall of the building was tottering and at the same time he saw a woman run out of the building onto the sidewalk. He tried to warn her of her danger, but as she did not move he rushed over toward her. Just then the whole front of the building fell out, and while the woman ran inside the doorway and was unharmed, Fenner was instantly killed..." Looking back, it soon became obvious that the only reason more people weren't killed by buildings collapsing into the streets was that it was so early in the morning.

A picture of Stockton St. from Union Square

Though most of the damage was centered in and around San Francisco, the quake itself was felt as far away as Los Angeles. Author Jack London felt it on his ranch in Glen Ellen and wrote to a family member, "Routed out of bed at a quarter past five. Half an hour later Mrs. London and I were in the saddle. We rode miles over the surrounding country. An hour after the shock, from a high place in the mountains, we could see at the same time the smoke of burning San Francisco and of burning Santa Rosa. Caught a train to Santa Rosa – Santa Rosa got it worse than S.F. Then in the afternoon, Wednesday afternoon, we got into San Francisco and spent the whole night in the path of the flames – you bet, I saw it all."

City Hall in ruins after the earthquake

Chapter 3: Help

"I was living with my family at 1310 Washington Street, near Jones, one of the most elevated parts of the city, and was awakened by the earthquake shock at 5:16 a.m...The entire street-car system being brought to a standstill by the damage resulting from the shock, I hastened on foot toward the business section of the city for the purpose of ascertaining what damage had been done to the hotels and other large buildings...I realized then that a great conflagration was inevitable, and that the city police force would not be able to maintain the fire-lines and protect public and private property over the great area affected. It was at once determined to order out all available troops not only for the purpose of guarding federal buildings, but to aid the police- and fire-departments of the city." - General Frederick Funston

Within minutes of the quake subsiding, General Frederick Funston, commander of nearby Fort Mason, knew that he and other leaders of the city were facing a catastrophe of epic proportions. He immediately dispatched a note to the fort ordering all available men to report for duty at the Hall of Justice and to put themselves as the disposal of Mayor Schmitz. His decisive thinking no doubt saved numerous lives and thousands of dollars in property, as it provided the city leaders with resources to get on top of the looting situation right away.

Funston

The troops arrived at around 7:00 a.m. and were quickly dispatched to patrol different parts of the city, and when a serious aftershock occurred at 8:14, they were on hand to help calm the public and manage the crowds milling about in panic. They would stay quite busy with crowd control as more than 130 more aftershocks shook the ground before the day was over. More soldiers arrived by boat from the headquarters of the First Battalion 22nd Infantry at around 10:00. A few minutes later, Admiral Casper Goodrich of the USS *Chicago* received a telegram informing him of the earthquake, and he quickly ordered his men to prepare to make way at full speed for the city. Only later would historians realized that this marked the first time the telegraph was used during a natural disaster.

The USS *Preble*, stationed out of Mare Island, was also on its way by this time and sent ashore a party of doctors and other medical personnel at around 10:30. After landing near the end of Howard Street, they acted as emergency treatment teams, caring for those injured until they could be taken to the Harbor Emergency Hospital. Their help was certainly needed, as Dr.

Blumer later recalled: "The third day I volunteered for work at the Harbor Emergency Hospital, the only undamaged one. This was because the Embarcadero between the city and the waterfront was so wide that the fire did not reach structures on the bay. During the 48 hours after the quake this hospital had a patient every two minutes. I recall seeing one patient with smallpox who was temporarily isolated out on a wharf, one sailor with a gunshot wound received while preventing looting, and a good many drug habitués, mostly courtesans from the Barbary Coast district, who could not get their morphine from the usual sources and would come to the hospital and beg for it."

What the soldiers saw when they arrived in the city was shocking even for the most battle hardened among them. What just a few hours earlier had been a thriving cultural and financial center now lay in ruins, the sounds of piano music and horse hooves having been replaced by an eerie silence punctuated by the moans of the injured and the screams of survivors searching for missing loved ones. In a world 40 years removed from large scale bombing attacks, no man there had ever seen anything like it. The commander of the *Chicago* later reported, "The city on the Fort Mason side of the harbor was, at this time, in full blaze. The buildings within the limits of the post were in danger. The air was filled with burning cinders which were blown by the wind far into the harbor and all the awnings on board had to be furled and the decks wet down to prevent fire. Thousands of panic stricken, homeless and destitute people thronged the shore in the neighborhood of the Fort. Food was being supplied but there had not yet been time for any well-organized system of distribution. Drinking water was difficult to find. All were eager to leave but no transportation was immediately available."

No one had time to stand around and take in the full magnitude of what they were seeing because fires were already breaking out around them, and there were still living people who could be rescued if they acted quickly. Most of all, there were throngs of panicked people determined to flee to the hills who had be managed. Bacigalupi ran into these crowds as he tried to make his way to his record store and described the chaos: "I hurried as much as possible, but did not make much headway owing to the fact that the majority of people were hurrying in the opposite direction to which I was going. They were taking to the hills. Some were dragging trunks; others carrying valises on their shoulders. I saw more talking machines in that one day than I believe I will ever see all together again in one time. It seems that the first thought of the owners of these machines was to save them in preference to anything else. There were also a great many comical sights such as a woman carrying ironing boards and an iron. One woman carried a parrot's cage in one hand, while in the other was a bundle of clothes, hurriedly gathered together. I noticed that the bottom of the cage was gone, having doubtlessly dropped out on the way without being missed."

A picture of residents along Market St. taken from the Ferry Building Tower

A picture of people trying to get out of the city

Chapter 4: Fire

Picture of the fire spreading near the Mission District

"On Wednesday morning at a quarter past five came the earthquake. A minute later the flames were leaping upward In a dozen different quarters south of Market Street, in the working-class ghetto, and in the factories, fires started. There was no opposing the flames. There was no organization, no communication. All the cunning adjustments of a twentieth century city had been smashed by the earthquake. The streets were humped into ridges and depressions, and piled with the debris of fallen walls. The steel rails were twisted into perpendicular and horizontal angles. The telephone and telegraph systems were disrupted. And the great water-mains had burst. All the shrewd contrivances and safeguards of man had been thrown out of gear by thirty seconds' twitching of the earth-crust." - Jack London

As destructive and deadly as the earthquake was, the worst destruction came not because of the buildings that fell but because of those that burned. Within moments of the tremors fading away, fires began to break out all over the city, caused and fed primarily by a combination of broken gas lines and open flames. Had other factors not aligned to allow their spread, the destruction still might have been held to a minimum, but the earthquake brought about the city's eventual decimation by limiting the method by which firemen could be dispatched. In his report, Fire Alarm Operator James Kelly explained, "Within a very few seconds after the shock ended I saw the smoke of an apparently large fire begin to rise from what I judged to be the vicinity of Market and Beale St. I at once went to key to strike out said box. No alarm came in for this fire, and be it noted that no alarms whatsoever came into the office after the commencement of the earthquake. Attempting to tap out as said, I at once found striker battery open. I rushed to battery room, saw battery jar broken; disconnected it and closed circuit; rushed back to key, found that I then had current on striker battery, but found the lines all open, and that I could not send signal out. Went then at once to the Tangent Galvanometer and tested out all of my lines, and found them all open."

To understand the magnitude of what Kelly wrote, it is important to note that a line was "open" if it was broken and not working. Furthermore, before he could attempt to trigger any other fire alarms, Kelly found himself battling a blaze in his own office: "The shock broke the chimney containing this fire place, and threw the fire out into the office. About the time I found my lines gone I tried to draw water from the faucets in the office to put out this fire, but found water gone. Water however flooded into the operating room in large quantities, and with this the fires were extinguished in the office." One can only imagine his angst as he watched the city he was charged with protecting go up in flames: "Within the next few minutes after noting the fire at Market and Beale Sts. as said, I counted five additional fires starting, at different points in view from the front windows of the office. One seemingly at California and Battery Sts.; one about Sacramento and Battery; another about Bush and Market, and the others in places which I did not so closely locate. About fifteen minutes after shock ceased, Battalion Chief McClusky called me up over a Police Box 'Phone, and asked me to send engines to Gas Works, as they had blown up. I told him of conditions, and that I could count some six fires toward the water front, and, giving him the general location of said fires, suggested that he get engines down to them if he could. He said all right, and within a short time I saw an engine coming, cutting its way through fallen wires and debris."

Kelly's reference to the debris in the roads explains the third cause of the fire damage, the fact that firefighters were unable to get to the blazes in a timely manner because broken walls and buildings were blocking the streets. Also, those streets that were not blocked by debris were often made just as impassable by the crowds of people fleeing the city. But ultimately, it was the lack of water to fight the fires that proved the most damning, because the same tremors that had broken the gas lines had also broken the waters lines. Again and again, firefighters would arrive at an area only to learn that the only water they had for battling the blaze was what they carried in their own tanks, and even that was soon drained.

That is not to say that there was no water at all to be had anywhere, especially early on. In his report, a fireman with the last name of Shaughnessy wrote, "At the fire which destroyed the building at the northwest corner of Mission and 22nd streets immediately after the earthquake, there was no water to be had east of Valencia Street, but the double hydrant at the northwest corner of 22nd and Valencia and the southwest corner of Valencia and 21st St. furnished an abundant supply, which, with the aid of the cistern at 22nd and Shotwell St., extinguished the fire. At the fire at the northwest corner of Hayes and Laguna streets, almost immediately after the earthquake, the water in the hydrant at that corner gave out after a few minutes, but a good supply was obtained at the corner of Buchanan and Hayes streets."

Naturally, the spreading fire caused even more hysteria among the public. One resident noted, "The fire was going on in the district south of them, and at intervals all night exhausted firefighters made their way to the plaza and dropped, with the breath out of them, among the huddled people and the bundles of household goods. The soldiers, who were administering affairs with all the justice of judges and all the devotion of heroes, kept three or four buckets of water, even from the women, for these men, who kept coming all night. There was a little food, also kept by the soldiers for these emergencies, and the sergeant had in his charge one precious bottle of whisky, from which is doled out drinks to those who were utterly exhausted. Over in a corner of the plaza a band of men and women were praying, and one fanatic, driven crazy by horror, was crying out at the top of his voice: 'The Lord sent it, the Lord!' His hysterical crying got on the nerves of the soldiers and bade fair to start a panic among the women and children, so the sergeant went over and stopped it by force. All night they huddled together in this hell, with the fire making it bright as day on all sides; and in the morning the soldiers, using their senses again, commandeered a supply of bread from a bakery, sent out another water squad, and fed the refugees with a semblance of breakfast."

Panoramic views of fires across San Francisco

Incredibly, one witness, a businessman named Jerome Clark, had taken a ferry into San Francisco after the earthquake, so he was on hand to describe the scene near the Bay:

"In every direction from the ferry building flames were seething, and as I stood there, a five-story building half a block away fell with a crash, and the flames swept clear across Market Street and caught a new fireproof building recently erected. The streets in places had sunk three or four feet, in others great humps had appeared four or five feet high. The street car tracks were bent and twisted out of shape. Electric wires lay in every direction. Streets on all sides were filled with brick and mortar, buildings either completely collapsed or brick fronts had just dropped completely off. Wagons with horses hitched to them, drivers and all, lying on the streets, all dead, struck and killed by the falling bricks, these mostly the wagons of the produce dealers, who do the greater part of their work at that hour of the morning. Warehouses and large wholesale houses of all descriptions either down, or walls bulging, or else twisted, buildings moved bodily two or three feet out of line and still standing with walls all cracked.

The Call building, a twelve-story skyscraper, stood and looked all right at first glance, but had moved at the base two feet at one end out into the sidewalk, and the elevators refused to work, all the interior being just twisted out of shape. It afterward burned as I watched it.

Fires were blazing in all directions, and all of the finest and best of the office and business buildings were either burning or surrounded. They pumped water from the bay, but the fire was soon too far away from the water front to make efforts in this direction of much avail. The water mains had been broken by the earthquake, and so there was no supply for the fire engines and they were helpless. The only way out was to dynamite, and I saw some of the finest and most beautiful buildings in the city, new modern palaces, blown to atoms. First they blew up one or two buildings at a time. Finding that of no avail, they took half a block; that was no use; then they took a block; but in spite of them all the fire kept on spreading."

Chapter 5: Water

"We obtained water here about 7 p.m., April 19th, and under the splendid leadership of Chief Murphy, of the 10th Battalion, S.F. Fire Department, we succeeded in checking the fire at this point and saving a block of buildings bounded on the North and West by Montgomery and Jackson Streets. The Appraisers' Building was in the next block to the Eastward, which was also saved at this time. The best work in my opinion, of the crews under my command, was done at this point. The fire chief had the assistance of but two of his own battalion and had no water. This was the only stream of water that ever reached this section of the city; and in feet this was the longest distance that any saltwater stream was taken from the water front -- the distance to the Leslie being a little over eleven blocks." - Lieutenant Frederick Freeman

It was only later, after fighting the first few fires used up their supplies, that the problem became a crisis. Again, Shaughnessy wrote, "The fire which started at Hayes and Gough, several hours after the earthquake, got beyond control by reason of there being no water available within reach, and it swept over the Western Addition east of Octavia and south of Golden Gate Ave.; crossed over Market St. near Ninth, and burned out into the Mission until finally stopped at Twentieth St…"

The firemen soon became very good at finding water, including pumping water from a large puddle caused by a break in the water main on what is now Van Ness Avenue, South. They also pumped water from household wells and commandeered the saltwater held in tanks by the United Railroads at Eleventh and Bryant Streets. One of the most disgusting accounts mentioned that "water was obtained for some time by draughting from the sewers, which were full of water from the broken mains at Seventh and Howard streets."

Of course, there were also a few natural sources of water as well. Shaughnessy mentioned, "The fire which started at Fifth and Minna streets and in the electric light works on Jessie St. near Third, which soon merged into one, were stopped from crossing Market St. by means of two small streams from the north side of Market St., where the pressure, ordinarily above 85 pounds, was about ten pounds."

The buildings nearest the docks were the easiest to save since the firefighters were able to pump an unlimited supply of seawater directly onto the fire, and this was what finally checked the fire damage done to the part of the city known as Chinatown. Home to thousands of hard-working Chinese immigrants who had come to the city to make a living by serving other Chinese arriving daily from around the country, it soon burned to the ground, in spite of the efforts of the firefighters to put out the blaze. The fire department would later be criticized for not fighting the fires in the part of town as hard as they had those in wealthier sections, but Shaughnessy's report details their efforts: "When the fire broke out in the Chinese wash house on Howard St. near Third, Engine Co. 4, whose quarters were across the street, could obtain no water from the hydrant, and was obliged to go to the cistern at Folsom and Second streets, from where a stream was obtained by doubling up with Engine Co. 10. This cistern was soon exhausted, and Engine 35 soon took the cistern at Folsom and First streets, and pumped to other engines, and after this was also exhausted Engine Co. 35 retired to the cistern at First and Harrison streets. The fire had reached such proportions, however, that this cistern, although having a capacity of 100,000 gallons, was drained without checking it, and the companies were forced to go to the foot of Third St., where by draughting from the Bay, the fire was prevented from crossing Townsend St."

Seawater also put out the flames at the end of Howard Street: "At Market and Beale streets, Engine Co. 1 obtained a little water for a short time, but nothing less than a dozen powerful streams could have stopped the fire that was in progress there. The same may be said of the fire that broke out at the same time at Stuart and Market streets, which, however, was checked at Howard St. by streams from the fire boats, assisted by two companies from Oakland."

By this time, both the firemen and their water supplies were becoming increasingly exhausted. Shaughnessy noted, "Engine Co. 1 also obtained water from the hydrant at Davis and California streets, and worked single-handed on a fire adjoining that corner for which, under ordinary conditions, a third alarm would have been sent in. In a short time this fire got beyond control and went to Market St. and the company was obliged to retire."

The story began to repeat itself over and over again; on Clay and Davis Streets, "no water was obtainable," so the firemen "retired to the cisterns at DuPont…All these cisterns were exhausted, while the fire was still advancing…" At Powell and California and Sacramento and Clay, Shaughnessy reported, "After a while these hydrants ran dry and the companies were forced to retire. Then the cistern at California and Mason streets was made use of in a desperate but unsuccessful effort to save the Hopkins Art Institute."

As they worked, the men became both more desperate and more discouraged. They lost City Hall to the "Hayes Valley Fire" but finally stopped it at Eddy Street. There were still working hydrants near the corner of Eddy and Van Ness, but the ones at Franklin Street were dry. When the fire at the Knickerbocker Hotel jumped the street and its sparks set fire to a building at the corner of California and Van Ness, Shaughnessy explained, "It was found that the nearest hydrant from which water could be obtained was at Bush and Laguna streets, and in order to reach the fire on California St., four engines had to be put in line. By the time this was done, the fire had crossed Sacramento and California streets and was burning up to Franklin St. in three blocks; when it was almost checked there, fire suddenly broke out in Kelly's stable on the south side of Pine St. near Franklin, and on account of the large frame buildings on the west side of Franklin St. there was great danger that the fire would cross that street and get beyond control."

Some of the most notorious incidents of the disaster truly put into perspective how helpless the city's officials felt when trying to battle the fires. A city resident named Adolphus Busch remembered, "The most terrible thing I saw was the futile struggle of a policeman and others to rescue a man who was pinned down in burning wreckage. The helpless man watched it in silence till the fire began burning his feet. Then he screamed and begged to be killed. The policeman took his name and address and shot him through the head." Max Fast recounted a similar tale: "When the fire caught the Windsor Hotel at Fifth and Market Streets there were three men on the roof, and it was impossible to get them down. Rather than see the crazed men fall in with the roof and be roasted alive the military officer directed his men to shoot them, which they did in the presence of 5,000 people."

Chapter 6: Dynamite

"By Wednesday afternoon, inside of twelve hours, half the heart of the city was gone. At that time I watched the vast conflagration from out on the bay. It was dead calm. Not a flicker of wind stirred. Yet from every side wind was pouring in upon the city. East, west, north, and south, strong winds were blowing upon the doomed city. The heated air rising made an enormous suck. Thus did the fire of itself build its own colossal chimney through the atmosphere. Day and night this dead calm continued, and yet, near to the flames, the wind was often half a gale, so mighty was the suck. Wednesday night saw the destruction of the very heart of the city. Dynamite was lavishly used, and many of San Francisco proudest structures were crumbled by man himself into ruins, but there was no withstanding the onrush of the flames. Time and again successful stands were made by the fire-fighters, and every time the flames flanked around on either side or came up from the rear, and turned to defeat the hard-won victory." - Jack London

It took three more engines to finally stop the spread of the fire at Sutter Street, but according to Shaughnessy, "Meanwhile the fire was spreading north unchecked on the east side of Van Ness Ave. until it reached Vallejo St., where Engine Co. 3, securing water from the hydrant at Green and Gough streets, and pumping to Engine Co. 20, fought the fire back to Polk St., only to lose its water at a critical time and be forced to move to Union and Gough." Finally, with the help of a fire boat supplied by the federal government, the fire was stopped at the corner of Union and Van Ness Avenue, but that was just one fire. Many others burned on, and even in recollection, Shaughnessy's report became more frantic: "In the meantime the fire was spreading over Russian Hill, and descending on the North Beach district. As there was not a drop of water in any of the mains, the companies were forced to resort to the remaining cisterns in that district, most of which had a capacity of only 20,000 gallons and were rapidly exhausted without materially checking the fire…A stream was also led from a Government boat at Filbert St. pier to Broadway and Powell streets, but without avail. The fire was then sweeping over Telegraph Hill rendering it impossible to reach the only unused cistern at DuPont and Greenwich streets, and the companies were forced to retire to the Seawall in a final effort to stay the conflagration. Streams were led up Stockton, Powell and Mason streets but the men were steadily driven back, until the fire worked around them to the west, and, driven by a strong west wind which had sprung up, swept down on the Seawall and forced them to beat a hasty retreat to Lombard St., where the fire on the water front was stopped with a stream from a boat, and the Merchants' Cold Storage plant was saved by the same means."

As the main water supplies were running out, the army came up with a new and radical solution for stopping the fire: using dynamite to destroy buildings standing in the fire's path. The idea was that these fallen buildings would create a sort of fire break that would spare the structures behind them. It was a radical and very controversial solution, but as the 18th wore on and the fires still burned, no one had any better ideas. Thus, the red batons of destruction were carefully transported from the California Powder Company at Pinole and carried to men who were expert in using them. Throughout the night, blast after blast lit up the sky, accompanied so often by shaking ground that people seemed to stop noticing it and little children slept soundly on.

In the years that followed, the army would be blamed for much of the destruction of the city. Many would say that the officers in charged had destroyed buildings unnecessarily and that all would have been well without their work. Others would point out that the use of the dynamite didn't really stop any of the fires and that they burned on anyway. However, those people had the benefit of hindsight and analysis, and it's not entirely fair to criticize people who were dealing with the disaster at the time and were ready to try anything.

Many would record their impressions of San Francisco bathed in the light of a thousand burning fires, but few did it as well as the famous author Jack London, who wrote, "Before the flames, throughout the night, fled tens of thousands of homeless ones. Some were wrapped in blankets. Others carried bundles of bedding and dear household treasures. Sometimes a whole family was harnessed to a carriage or delivery wagon that was weighted down with their possessions. Baby buggies, toy wagons, and go-carts were used as trucks, while every other person was dragging a trunk. Yet everybody was gracious. The most perfect courtesy obtained. Never in all San Francisco's history, were her people so kind and courteous as on this night of terror…All night these tens of thousands fled before the flames. Many of them, the poor people from the labor ghetto, had fled all day as well. They had left their homes burdened with possessions. Now and again they lightened up, flinging out upon the street clothing and treasures they had dragged for miles."

Ultimately, the dynamite didn't do much good and the fires raged on until they burned themselves out four days after the earthquake. By that time, thousands of people had died and millions of dollars in property had been lost. In fact, one historian estimates that the value of the property lost in the city was approximately equivalent to the budget of the entire federal government that year. What is known is that the earthquake and fires combined to destroy nearly 500 city blocks and 25,000 buildings, leaving over a quarter of a million people homeless.

A picture of Market St. laying in ruins

Picture of the ruins of Fourth St. just off Market St.

Chapter 7: Martial Law

A depiction of Army soldiers providing goods to San Francisco

Soldiers standing among the ruins

Soldiers pose outside the Hall of Justice

"Throughout this whole day constant trouble had been experienced owing to the large number of drunken people along the waterfront. My force was unarmed with the exception of the officers, who carried revolvers; and the police, of whom I only saw two, were absolutely helpless. The crowds rushed saloon after saloon and looted the stocks becoming intoxicated early in the day. In my opinion great loss of life resulted from men and women becoming stupefied by liquor and being too tired and exhausted to get out of the way of the fire. During this whole day we needed unarmed men to rescue women and children in the neighborhood of Rincon Hill, the fire having made a clean sweep of this poor residence district in about an hour's time. The most heartrending sights were witnessed in this neighborhood, but with my handful of men we could not do as much for the helpless as we wished. Able-bodied men refused to work with the fire department, stating that they would not work for less than forty cents an hour, etc. Men refused to aid old and crippled men and women out of the way of the fire and only thought of themselves." - Lieutenant Frederick Freeman

Society likes to believe that a disaster brings out the best in people, and it often does. Arnold Genthe, who had been at the opera house the night before, told of his breakfast the morning of the disaster: "Inside the hotel…there was no gas or electricity, but somehow hot coffee was available which, with bread and butter and fruit, made a satisfying breakfast. When I asked the waiter for a check he announced with a wave of his hand, 'No charge today, sir. Everyone is welcome as long as things hold out.'"

At the same time, panic and terror also bring out the worst in people, and that was why, while many of the soldiers and sailors dispatched to San Francisco kept busy working to put out fires and dig out those who were trapped, others had their hands full trying to keep order. There were a number of problems keeping law enforcement officers busy. The first and most pressing issue was trying to rescue those who were trapped, but while there were also a few good Samaritans who pitched in to help look for survivors, most people were too concerned about their own safety and that of their families to take an active interest in others. Others insisted that they would only work if paid for their labor, and paid well at that.

The second issue was the swelling masses of people taking to the streets and trying to get out of town. Bailey Millard described one scene: "Automobiles piled high with bedding and hastily snatched stores, tooted wild warnings amid the crowds. Drays loaded with furniture and swarming over with men, women and children, struggled over the earthquake-torn street, their horses sometimes falling by the wayside in a vain effort to pass some bad fissure in the 'made' ground. Cabs, for which fares at the rate of ten to twenty dollars apiece had been paid in advance, dotted the procession, and there were vans, express wagons of all sorts, buggies and carts, all loaded down with passengers and goods."

On April 20, the USS *Chicago* rescued more than 20,000 people who had run toward the harbor while trying to escape the spreading fire. The ships spent the entire day sailing back and forth across San Francisco Bay, ferrying as many people as it could safely carry across to safer shores. It remains the largest evacuation of a civilian population by sea in history and rivals the more famous evacuation of Dunkirk that took place during World War II.

The third problem was how to feed and care for the large number of people who did not make it out of the city. The crisis of food and shelter fell on the wealthy and the poor alike, as it did not matter how much food one might have had at home once the homes were gone. Funston sent out a request for food and tents to all nearby military establishments, and the following morning, he received word from the Secretary of State, William Howard Taft, that all the tents the United States Army had to spare were on their way to San Francisco.

Ernest Adams, a respected citizen, observed "The city is under martial law and we are living on the government, or at least many are. As soon as the good were safe, I cleaned out the nearest grocery store of canned goods and we are living in tents, cooking meals on a few bricks piled up Dutch-oven style." Another man, David Hill, described the lives of the newly homeless: "When daylight came we helped cook our breakfast in the street where rich and poor alike squat side by side cooking on brick stoves, and then all go stand in line to get their share of provisions. No one is allowed to sell a thing there but everything left in stores has been distributed, and loads are coming in every day."

Picture of a camp that housed refugees

Picture of refugees in front of a tent

The fourth and most dangerous issue surrounded how to protect private property. At 3:00 on the afternoon of the 18th, Mayor Schmitz met with the city leader to appoint a "Committee of Fifty" made up of men he trusted to lead San Francisco in a time of crisis. During the meeting, he stated emphatically, "Let it be given out that three men have already been shot down without mercy for looting. Let it also be understood that the order has been given to all soldiers and policemen to do likewise without hesitation in the cases of any and all miscreants who may seek to take advantage of the city's awful misfortune." As good as his word, he followed up that statement with handbills that were tacked up all over town. They read:

> "The Federal Troops, the members of the Regular Police Force and all Special Police Officers have been authorized by me to KILL any and all persons found engaging in Looting or in the Commission of Any Other Crime.
>
> I have directed all the Gas and Electric Lighting Co.'s not to turn on Gas or Electricity until I order them to do so. You may therefore expect the city to remain in darkness for an indefinite time.

I request all citizens to remain at home from darkness until daylight every night until order is restored.

I WARN all Citizens of the danger of fire from Damaged or Destroyed Chimneys, Broken or Leaking Gas Pipes or Fixtures, or any like cause."

While his order seems extreme, it was not challenged by anyone in authority when it was put into place. In fact, some might say that it was too strictly enforced. David Hill later recalled of that first night: "At 5 o'clock a rifle shot was heard on the block and some young fellow fell dead who was imprudent enough to venture out to borrow some whiskey for his sick mother. A soldier ordered him to throw it away and shot him for refusing. This is only one of many cases."

A picture of soldiers looting pairs of shoes in the middle of Market St.

Chapter 8: Burning Bigotry

"One of the evils springing from the late disaster to San Francisco…is the great influx of Chinese into this city from San Francisco. Not only have they pushed outward the limits of Oakland's heretofore constricted and insignificant Chinatown, but they have settled themselves in large colonies throughout the residence parts of the city, bringing with them their vices and their filth. The residence of C.H. King…has been leased to Chinese, and now the house is crowded with Mongolians, 60 or 70 occupying the premises. Already this house…has taken on the air of a Chinese hangout. It is a rendezvous for scores of Celestials, who shuffle in and out of the place, for what purpose, one familiar with their life can easily conjecture. The residents of the neighborhood, many of them members of Oakland's most exclusive society, are up in arms, and will appeal to the authorities to abate this nuisance." - *The Oakland Herald*, April 27, 1906

    Once the fires were out and the city began to think of rebuilding, the underlying issue of racism surfaced. For decades, San Francisco had been the home of a large number of Chinese immigrants, and in keeping with the standards of the time, they mostly lived in Chinatown. However, the fire destroyed that section of town and left most of its citizens just as homeless as the wealthiest white politicians. At first, there were rumors that the Asian-Americans were not receiving the same number and quality of rations as were their white neighbors, an issue so scandalous that it was reported in the newspapers back east and led to a directive straight from the White House that everyone be cared for equally.

    However, by the time the directive made its way through to San Francisco, most of the people in question had left town and headed to nearby Oakland, where they were able to use their culture's famous familial ties to find places to live. As the shocking quote above demonstrates, Oakland's own bigotry cried out against this influx of immigrants, but San Francisco soon cried out against it as well, albeit for different reasons. According to an article in the *San Francisco Chronicle* on May 2, 1906, entitled *Now Fear That The Chinese May Abandon City*, "Charles S. Wheeler informed the committee [on Chinese affairs] that he had been in consultation with the first secretary of the Chinese legation on the preceding day, and cautioned the committee, before taking any action, to look well into the future and inform itself thoroughly as to what influence its action might have on the future of San Francisco. He declared that if the situation were not wisely handled the bulk of San Francisco's Oriental trade might be diverted to other Pacific Coast ports. Seattle was making a strong bid for this trade, he declared, and would like to welcome the Chinese of this city. By the exercise of caution and diplomacy, he thought San Francisco might still retain its large Oriental trade, and at the same time look after its own civic affairs."

    As always, it was that last bit about "look after its own civic affairs" that presented the problem. San Francisco saw its "civic affairs" as primarily serving the needs of it wealthy white population. The city leaders also knew that the section of the city that had previously housed Chinatown was prime real estate that others had wanted to get their hands on for years. Thus, they were anxious to try to pick a new, less attractive section of the city to offer to Chinese residents when they returned. This would prove to be a problem that would get the attention of everyone from the mayor to the President of the United States and even the royal family of China. Fortunately, a satisfactory arrangement was found, and the Asian-Americans returned to

San Francisco to eventually become a valued part of society.

Moreover, there were those in the community who were not just willing to help the Chinese in their city but had been doing so for years. The Occidental Board Mission Home for Chinese Girls was run by the famous missionary Donaldina Cameron. She remained as devoted to her charges, many of whom had been rescued from slavery, on that day as she had all the other days she had been in charge of the home. Though their building survived, they were soon forced to evacuate the premises because of approaching fire. Cameron later wrote, "To have our Chinese girls on the streets among these crowds after nightfall was a danger too great to risk. As hastily, therefore, as we could work amidst the confusion and excitement, we gathered some bedding, a little food, and a few garments together and the last of the girls left the Mission Home. They tramped the long distance to Van Ness Avenue carrying what they could. On the way the children joined the party, and the entire family was at last established for the night in the Presbyterian Church ... the small children and babies were carefully cared for through all the excitement. There were three babies— the tiny Ah Ping, not a month old, had to be tenderly carried by the girls; her poor little mother (a rescued slave) was too feeble and helpless to aid much. Hatsu had her wee baby, only three months old, and little Ah Chung, eighteen months, was equally helpless..."

Donaldina Cameron

The next morning, they made one last trip to the mission house, which the fire had not yet reached, and got what provisions they could carry out. From there, they set out on the long journey, on foot, to the ferry, where they successfully pleaded for passage across to the Seminary at San Anselmo. She later described their will to go on by writing, "As tears would not avail…laughter was the tonic which stimulated that weary, unwashed, and uncombed procession on the long tramp through stifling, crowded streets near where the fire raged, and through the desolate district already burned, where fires of yesterday still smoldered."

Chapter 9: Rising from the Ashes

Panoramic views of San Francisco in ruins

Aerial view of San Francisco's remains

"The earthquake period is gone. Once the pent up forces of nature have had a vent, nothing of a serious nature need be apprehended. At the most a succession of minor shocks may be felt and that's all. It is not unreasonable, therefore, for people to continue in dread of a new destructive temblor. People should fearlessly go to work and repair mischief done and sleep quietly at night anywhere at all, especially in wooden frame. Never mind foreboders of evil: they do not know what they are talking about. Seismonetry is in its infancy and those therefore who venture out with predictions of future earthquakes when the main shock has taken place ought to be arrested as disturbers of the peace." - Father Ricard, April 22, 1906

Even in the midst of the disaster, many businessmen were as worried about their inventories as they were their lives. Within a week of the disaster, Ernest Adams had contacted his superiors at the famous Reed and Barton silver company and given them a full report of all he did to save their inventory: "Reaching the office, I waded through plaster, etc., to find the goods still in the cases but off the shelves without any damage being done them. Locking the doors again I rushed to street...I gathered up a force of seven men, stationed them at our office doors, and started for a truck...Fortunately I had two guns in the office, and stationing one man at the entrance and one on the truck with orders to shoot, the balance of us went to work, and that dray man pulled the heaviest load of his life. I saved all of the Sterling Hollow and Flat Ware with the exception of a few Flat Ware samples in the trays beside my books, stock sterling and plated ware books. The plated ware, it was impossible to touch, as the flames were then upon us...."

Adams went on to devote himself to protecting his prized inventory, hauling it from place to place and keeping it in his personal possession until he was able to once more secure it in a shop: "All Wednesday night we guarded the treasure, but the fire kept creeping toward us, driving the people back to the Cliff House, the western extremity of the Peninsula, and Thursday I was again forced to move the goods westward. The last stand was our back yard, two miles from the first stand, and I am now with our sterling goods, the remains of our beautiful office. The city is under martial law and we are living on the government, or at least many are…With this valuable property under my care I could not afford to take any chances, and I have stayed close to my cache."

Mr. Bacigalupi had even more concern for his business, since his inventory of phonograph records and musical instruments was a huge investment on his part: "I ran down to my store, trying to unfasten the door, but the lock was so hot [from the approaching fire] that in trying to unfasten same I scorched my fingers. I worked for what seemed to be an hour, but which in reality must have been from twenty to thirty seconds." After finally getting inside, he was surprised and grieved by what he saw: "You can imagine my feelings on going to the second floor where my Phonograph salesroom was located, and seeing every Record standing on its shelf in perfect order, just as though there had been no earthquake at all…to think that the Pianos had been thrown down on their faces, and Records, which stood by the thousands on our shelves, had not been moved."

In spite of the loss of his five story building and a lot its contents, Bacigalupi was able to recognize the opportunity that the disaster was offering him. He wrote to a friend that "while the fire was still burning close to the store from which I am now writing, I secured this good location at a nominal cost for my Phonograph business. One week later I was offered three times what I am paying for rent, but I refused. I am now engaged in the real estate business; have opened a market place two blocks from the main street of New 'Frisco, and am also interested in a restaurant, cigar stand, and last and most important of all—the Phonograph business…I have decided to use this store, which is centrally located, in which to retail talking machines of all the leading makes, and am putting up my own building on leased ground, two blocks from here, in which to conduct the business of jobbing Edison Phonographs, which has been my chief occupation for the last eight years." Understanding that those to whom he was writing might be surprised by his decision to start again from scratch at 51 years old, he added, "I am game, and intend to go to it now as I did then. I have taken into the firm my two sons, with the aid of whom I believe I will be able to do a better and larger business in talking machines than has ever been done in the West…Regardless of all those ordeals I AM GOING TO STICK WITH 'FRISCO."

Many others would join him in "sticking with 'Frisco." Surprisingly to some, most of the people that had lived in the community before the disaster moved back into their homes as soon as they were given the all clear. Their reasons for staying were as varied as their individual backgrounds, but many had no choice because they were too poor to be able to afford to move anywhere else. Others, like Bacigalupi, saw an opportunity to make a profit from rebuilding.

People like Bacigalupi turned out to be mostly right, because the city did rise from the ashes at an incredible rate. Within a decade, San Francisco was bigger and more prosperous than it had ever been before. Arnold Genthe was a witness to that rebirth: "Among the many telegrams I received was one from Edward Sothern and Julia Marlowe. 'Now that you have lost everything,' it read, 'you should come to New York. We will see that you find a fully equipped studio waiting for you, so that you can start work without delay.' It was heartening and consoling to have this fine proof of real friendship. The temptation was great, but I was not willing to leave San Francisco then. I wanted to stay, to see the new city which would rise out of the ruins. I felt that my place was there. I had something to contribute, even if only in a small measure, to the rebuilding of the city. I started my search for a new studio. It would take years before the business section would be rebuilt. No one knew exactly just where the new center of the city was to be. Location was unimportant. On Clay Street, not far from the gates of the Presidio I discovered a picturesque one-story cottage. In its small garden was a fine old scrub-oak, and I believe it was this and not so much the house that made me decide to take a five-year lease. My friends encouraged me. 'Don't worry about being so far out. We'll come anyway, no matter where you are. The chief thing is for you to have a place that you like and where…you can work.' And so I started to make a few structural changes and to get together the necessary equipment that would enable me to continue my work as a portrait photographer."

Some people saw the earthquake as source of spiritual inspiration. Just like those who fell to their knees in prayer as the city shook down around them, so they continued to look to strength from a higher power throughout their experience. To them, the earthquake was yet another opportunity to find truth and beauty in a fallen world. One such woman was Emma Burke, who later wrote that "this stupendous disaster leads a thoughtful person to two conclusions: viz., faith in humanity; and the progress of the human race. All artificial restraints of our civilization fell away with the earthquake's shocks. Every man was his brother's keeper. Everyone spoke to everyone else with a smile. The all-prevailing cheerfulness and helpfulness were encouraging signs of our progress in practicing the golden rule, and humanity's struggle upward toward the example of our Savior."

Of course, the reason most people stayed was as simple as it was meaningful: San Francisco was home. Many of them had come west as young men searching for gold. Some of them had found it, and many stayed to help build up the city. The 49ers were now old men and disinclined to start over anywhere else. Others had come to the city from the other side of the world and had worked hard for years to raise enough money to bring their families to join them. They dreamed of a time when they could leave their small businesses to their sons and grandsons. Many had been born in the city and knew no other place to live. They were just as determined to rebuild the city itself as they were their own homes.

Howard Livingston, speaking decades later, described his family's life in the aftermath of the disaster, and how their belief in their city's ultimate destiny drove them back into the town rather than away from it: "A few days after the fire ended, my mother and the younger children returned to our home, and I found work at the warehouse of a wholesale drug company which opened in a temporary location. Everyone was busy, and I frequently heard people say that the new San Francisco would be a far finer city than the one which had been destroyed. Some weeks later the Vulcan Iron Works reopened, and I found employment in their structural steel department. I worked on the steel framing of some of the first new buildings erected after the fire. Five generations of my family have lived in San Francisco. It is a city for which I feel great affection, and I have always been glad that I was able to have a small part in its rebuilding."

Bibliography

Aitken, Frank W.; Edward Hilton (1906). A History Of The Earthquake And Fire In San Francisco. San Francisco: The Edward Hilton Co.

Banks, Charles Eugene; Opie Percival Read (1906). The History Of The San Francisco Disaster And Mount Vesuvius Horror. C. E. Thomas.

Bronson, William (1959). *The Earth Shook, the Sky Burned*. Doubleday.

Double Cone Quarterly, Fall Equinox, volume VII, Number 3 (2004).

Greely, Adolphus W. (1906). Earthquake In California, April 18, 1906. Special Report On The Relief Operations Conducted By The Military Authorities. Washington: Government Printing Office.

Jordan, David Starr; John Casper Branner, Charles Derleth, Jr., Stephen Taber, F. Omari, Harold W. Fairbanks, Mary Hunter Austin (1907). *The California Earthquake of 1906*. San Francisco: A. M. Robertson.

Keeler, Charles (1906). San Francisco Through Earthquake And Fire. San Francisco: Paul Elder And Company.

London, Jack. "The Story of an Eyewitness". London's report from the scene. Originally published in Collier's Magazine. May 5, 1906.

Morris, Charles (1906). The San Francisco Calamity By Earthquake And Fire

Schussler, Hermann (1907). The Water Supply Of San Francisco, California Before, During And After The Earthquake of April 18, 1906 And The Subsequent Conflagration. New York: Martin B. Brown Press.

Tyler, Sydney; Harry Fielding Reid (1908, 1910). *The California Earthquake of April 18, 1906: Report of The State Earthquake Investigation Commission, Volumes I and II*. Washington, D.C.: The Carnegie Institution of Washington.

Tyler, Sydney; Ralph Stockman Tarr (1908). San Francisco's Great Disaster. Philadelphia: P. W. Ziegler Co.

Wald, David J.; Kanamori, Hiroo; Helmberger, Donald V.; Heaton, Thomas H. (1993), "Source study of the 1906 San Francisco Earthquake", *Bulletin of the Seismological Society of America* (Seismological Society of America) **83** (4): 981–1019

Winchester, Simon, *A Crack in the Edge of the World: America and the Great California Earthquake of 1906*. HarperCollins Publishers, New York, 2005.

The 1989 Bay Area Earthquake

Chapter 1: Mother Nature Plays Ball

"DISPATCHER: Oh, my God, we're having an earthquake – wait a minute, hold on – hold on. Can you feel that?

CALLER: Yes, I sure can.

DISPATCHER: Okay, this is interesting. There go the lights. Oh, s–t! (clamor of metal dispatch consoles rattling and banging in background before tape stops from power failure.)" – Transcript from a 911 call after the earthquake

Like so many other natural disasters, earthquakes do not typically arrive without some warning. In most cases, the warnings consist of some gentle tremors felt during the days leading up to the big event, and this was true in California in 1989. Before October 17, 1989, there was a series of small tremors that were felt in the days leading up to the big event, but Bay Area residents were already accustomed to a few shakes from time to time. In fact, in the six years leading up to the October 17, 1989 quake, California was struck by 11 other significant earthquakes along the famous San Andreas fault, and earthquakes had long been seen as a part of life in the state, much like hurricanes along the Florida coasts or blizzards in Alaska. They went with the territory, and those who chose to live in California likewise chose to prepare as best they could for the inevitable.

Though it wasn't a warning in the strictest sense, some residents noticed a dramatic change in the weather ahead of the earthquake and took note of it. Eve Iverson, an Army Reserve officer assigned to the nearby Presidio, observed, "The temperature had climbed ten degrees from the day before and the humidity had built to a level that many would remember as sultry. As the fans waited in their seats at Candlestick Park some complained that 83 F was hot, especially for October 17, 1989. The lack of wind at Candlestick Park was all the more remarkable since if any kind of breeze was blowing it would make itself felt in the stadium. To the philosopher Aristotle these conditions were the precursor to a temblor. Geologists had long ago disproved any link between weather and seismic activity but the old concept had hardened into a cliché."

Another problem with anticipating an earthquake is that it was often "earthquake weather" in

California, just like there were also often small tremors. Many of the same natural phenomena that first attracted settlers to the area in search of gold or lush land on which to grow crops and raise cattle made the area susceptible to earthquakes. Thus, any major concerns about an imminent earthquake of high magnitude were not enough to cancel two important events, as Iverson noted: "The next evening The California Academy of Sciences had the first of a two-part lecture scheduled on 'Earthquakes–Faulty Facts and Shaky Myths.' It was a presentation that would have to wait while Nature gave its own geology lesson. The baseball season was ending with the World Series to be played between the San Francisco Giants and the Oakland Athletics. The first two games had been held at the Oakland Coliseum with the home team winning. At approximately 5 PM the third game was to begin at Candlestick."

Without a doubt, the strongest sense of anticipation that evening was not over an impending quake but an impending ball game. Diane Langdon was in the stadium that night with her husband David. Both officers in the United States Army and members of the Military Police Force, they were looking forward to joining their fellow officers in carrying flags into the Opening Ceremonies that were about to begin. Diane Langdon later recalled, "It was a really hot day, but it hadn't been hot in the morning, so some of us had taken sweaters. As we were going down the Great Highway SFC Pellegato said. 'Look at the water, it looks like the calm before the storm. Can you believe how calm it is?' We didn't think anything of it, we just said 'yeah.' It was very hot and the bus was hot and we were all antsy ... it was just so hot."

Her husband David made a similar observation: "As we drove down, everyone commented on how hot it was, how calm the winds were, how quiet the Bay was, the stillness of the water, the old proverb, 'The calm before the storm' type of thing. It was rather scenic, in my opinion, but the relatively calm water of the Bay and then the lack of wind for October was unusual from what I was told."

In fact, a number of people were concerned about an earthquake striking during the game. Carol Bold, a native San Franciscan, explained, "The 1989 World Series was also taking place at this time. The Oakland Athletics and San Francisco Giants were battling it out down at Candlestick Park. In fact there was even a columnist by the name of Kevin Cowherd of the Baltimore Sun who had already predicted the earthquake just that morning. In The San Jose Mercury News he wrote, 'these are two teams from California and God only knows if they'll ever get all the games in. An earthquake could rip through the Bay Area before they sing the anthem for Game 3.' And that was precisely when the earthquake struck. I don't know if his column could be construed as irony, or just dumb chance. In any event there's probably not much use overanalyzing it. The game was postponed for ten days though, so I guess he was right about a lot of things."

Indeed, not long after people had arrived at the stadium, right around 5:04 p.m., the earthquake hit. Diane and David were right in the middle of getting organized for the big parade into the stadium, and initially, Diane did not know what was happening. When she realized the area was being hit by an earthquake, it was hard for her to believe. She described the pandemonium in the stadium: "There was a loud noise and we looked up to see a plane going overhead and then in a split second it started shaking; it was like the plane was causing the shaking - but no, that's not the plane, it's an earthquake. The next thing I knew I felt it hit my feet, not knowing whether to go to the left or right, I actually looked down on the ground to see whether or not there was a crack between my feet that's how strong it felt. Above us, to the left the light stanchions were swaying, not just shaking, they were swaying back and forth. The concrete on the upper deck moved apart and you could see the sky on the other side. No one fell but you could see the sections of concrete moving apart and then back together. There wasn't panic we stood there and I thought 'Oh my God, man, what a day! Some timing!'"

Standing near his wife, David stared in awe as everything around him shook and wobbled. He would later learn that the earthquake was one of the most powerful of the 20th century, registering a 6.9 on the famous Richter scale. However, at that moment, all he noticed was the way in which the stadium itself seemed to split apart before his very eyes: "The spooky part of it was looking up in the stands, completely full. Imagine Candlestick Park completely coming apart and going back together. To see the slabs above the upper deck separate by feet and come back together, and watch the light stanchions sway left and right from the apex to the center, about fifteen feet either way, it was a sight to behold, if you've never seen it. Then to look out to the field and just see it roll as if it were an ocean, because it was moving like a wave, just like water; waves and waves and waves. Before panic could set in, it stopped, all within about ten to fifteen seconds. Fans reacted really great; they applauded at first thinking that this is San Francisco and it would be apropos to have an earthquake during the World Series. Until we found out the devastation it had done. [When the shaking stopped] the announcement said that people in the lower decks go to the middle of the field, people in the upper deck get out by the stairway."

Of course, the Langdon's were only two of the thousands of people present that day. With a capacity for 60,000 spectators and an estimated 30,000 already in the stadium, it was something of a miracle that no one was seriously injured or killed. One man who was up in the stands at the stadium that day later shared his experience, writing that he "was at World Series game when Candlestick got hit at just after 5 p.m. on that terrible Tuesday. I was standing at the end of a first base tunnel looking down on the field when I heard what sounded like a large jet descending on SF International. But suddenly everything started shaking and the light standards started swaying and I grabbed a railing so as not to lose my footing and balance. When the tremor was over, I noticed that half of the stadium lights were out and that pieces of cement were strewn about. And then many of us in the crowd saw the plume of smoke rising from S.F. and knew that all was not well. And later it was also not so well trying to drive back (in the dark except for car lights) to Oakland by way of San Jose where, thankfully, the city lights shone brightly. A memorable but harrowing experience to say the least."

In addition to the adults, some of whom had come to California from all over the country, there were many young people in the stadium who were anxious to see their first World Series game. Christy Scherrer was a young girl looking forward to watching the game with her father when the quake hit, but excitement later turned to terror when their route home took them through a part of the city being overrun by rioting looters. She later wrote, "I was at the game. My dad caught a woman as she fainted in front of him and chunks of cement were falling. It was a slow chaos as we started to see the smoke from the fire and heard report that 'the bridge had fallen' from people who had radios or 'watchmans' with them. As the freeway entrances were closed, we drove through the Bayview. As the bottles and bricks whirled toward our car, my father told my brother and I to duck down as low as we could as he was sure the windshield would eventually shatter. The freeway was not a possible way home and we drove from SF to Los Altos on El Camino the whole way. Many cars ran out of gas...we didn't. It took us six hours to make it 40 miles home. I am still nervous, 24 years later, to see my gas tank dip below half a tank."

Of course, as many people as there were watching the game at Candlestick, many more were in front of their television sets at home. In fact, millions of people from around the world would have the unusual experience of seeing an earthquake on television as it was taking place. One young man later recalled, "I was just about to sit down in my living room in Willow Glen at the time when it started to shake and the game just blacked out. The exposed ceiling above me began to creak loudly as the wooden planks rocked from side to side. I jumped up and went to stand in my front doorway and looked north up Lincoln Ave and had that 'Oh ****!' moment when I saw the street rolling up and down in waves as car alarms went off. My roommates and I moved the sofa onto the lawn and drank beer the rest of the afternoon and waved at traffic as it crawled by....when the power came back on, I was convinced that SF was destroyed."

Chapter 2: A Blow to San Francisco

Picture of a crack that formed in a roadway during the earthquake

"Dispatcher: 911 San Francisco Emergency

Caller: Emergency, I reside at 1782 Fifteenth Street and, as you know, there was a severe earthquake. But, I'm concerned about someone that's sitting outside and the person is in total shock. She won't say anything to anybody, she's just crying. She's in shock and we don't know what to do for her.

Dispatcher: Okay ma'am, the best thing is go wrap a blanket around her. There's not a whole lot we can do. I've got to get off this line and see if there's anybody else who needs help. Go out there and wrap a blanket around her, and remember to stay in doorways and under solid things, okay?

Caller: Okay." - Transcript from a 911 call after the earthquake

Although the scenes from Candlestick remain the most famous aspect of the earthquake, it was doing severe damage all across San Francisco. Army Firefighter Vincent Milano was at his station when the earthquake hit and described the scene there: "Everything just started shaking, rocking, whatever it was. We always thought our station was a rocking station-we play our music loud-but [this time we] shook. Actually, it was kind of fun at the time, [at least] I thought it was, I was so used to it being here all my life and going through earthquakes. After it stopped, Captain Haggerty immediately told us to get the equipment out of the station, [in case] the building is unstable or doors are not able to open. We just wanted to get everything out so we would be able to use it. Captain Smith was trying to come down during the earthquake, he was pretty much thrown around the stairs left and right. Every time he would try to go down, he got thrown back up. The dispatcher was Darryl Barr, he immediately came back into the Communications Center and took over. He tried to make sense of everything that was going on here. There was confusion at the time."

Nearby, Military Policeman Kurt Mercier was working out at the gym near his base at the Presidio, but while he was lifting weights, he realized something strange was going on: "It started out with little vibrations under the feet, you hear a little shaking going on, and it started getting harder and harder. You could bear a roaring sound, weights started to fall off the racks, the electricity went out, cutting all the lights and making the gym totally dark. I tried to walk. I was thrown down, just as though the floor was buckling. When it finally settled down someone made it to the door ...and let some light inside."

Although it was just after 5:00, many people in the city were still at work. Some were staying late to finish up a project, while others were just waiting for some of the traffic to die down. One woman who was asked about her experience refused to give her name because she was caught in a rather awkward position by the tremors: "I was at work in the basement bathroom of a large jewelry store in Union Square. In the middle of Number 1, I felt a slight rumble, and then the lights went out. Making my way upstairs was tricky. All of the staff was just standing around confused and wondering what to do. We got excused for the day. The buses were jam-packed and inching across Mission Street. Cars were crossing intersections timidly. I decided to walk home to the Excelsior. It was like walking after the apocalypse--shell-shocked zombies, insane traffic, debris, and a general pervasive feeling of fear. I was followed by a creepy guy for a few miles who got hostile when I finally confronted him. Fortunately I was able to lose him when it got dark and made it home about 8:00 p.m. Still, I had it way better than those poor people who died in their homes in the Marina and on the bridge."

A picture of rubble in the Marina district

As embarrassing as being caught with one's pants down in a bathroom was, there were far more dangerous places to be when the quake hit, as Michael Bello soon learned: "I was an Interior Design student at Academy of Art College located on Northpoint Street across from Pier 39. ... I took the elevator to the second floor just in time...I walked in alone and as the elevator situated itself on the floor. A sharp jolt shook it...feeling as if people where fighting outside and had pushed it...and within seconds the whole elevator shook vigorously for how many seconds and it continued, and the lights went off as the door opened for about 6 inches...just enough for me to pry it open. As I manually opened it ajar...all I can see was darkness in the hallways, sound of fire alarm ringing, students screaming to evacuate the building...! There were areas where the sprinkler system activated that got everyone wet! We all ran down the emergency exits and spilled out on the streets. What we thought was just a strong quake, ended up being a devastating earthquake as people huddled by cars and listened to the news."

There are several colleges and universities in the San Francisco area, so, like Bello, many of those affected by the quake were students. One young man later remembered, "I was in the basement law journal office of Hastings Law School at McAllister and Hyde. At first, we all thought the quake was the usual rumbling of some storage carts immediately above the office, but we quickly realized what was going on. The ground beneath felt like Jello. Being in a basement of a building is bad enough, with the whole thing swaying above you, but then the lights went out as well leaving us in total darkness (the emergency lights did not come on as they were supposed to). Somebody had a lighter, and we all followed him, single file, up the stairs to daylight. The next couple of hours or so were spent in speculation about the Bay Bridge 'collapsing,' as reported by Dan Rather and others. News did not travel as fast in those days as it does now."

Pictures of a damaged building and a crushed car in the Marina district

Many of the young people studying in San Francisco had come to the city from other parts of the country and were not accustomed to tremors, so the 1989 earthquake was both shocking and terrifying. One such student explained, "I was attending San Francisco State and was walking under Hensill Hall towards Stonestown. (anyone that is familiar with Hensill Hall could imagine how scary that was being under it!). Looked up and saw a large crack forming right before my eyes above my head! I started running toward 19th Ave, but wasn't quite sure why. I didn't realize it was actually an earthquake until I heard some guy yelling, 'that's the biggest…earthquake I ever felt!' I thought a MUNI car [the San Francisco transportation system] had hit the side of one of the buildings on campus. People were pouring out of Stonestown. I drove along Sunset Blvd. All the traffic lights were out. Radio news said the Bay Bridge had collapsed. Very little information. Then heard the Cyprus Freeway in Oakland had also collapsed. Total shock and disbelief. Phone lines were all busy. Got home…no power…neighbors listening to battery powered radios outside. A day and week I'll never forget! Had no shops to go to, no restaurants open, no schools open…everything closed up…nothing! The entire city was dark with the exception of the burning orange glow from the fires in the Marina."

Picture of a damaged building in the Marina district

Others in the city that day knew what it was like to endure an earthquake. For instance, one woman knew that her life was about to get significantly busier as soon as she felt the quake hit: "I was a nurse at Kaiser Hospital San Francisco. My patient felt the earthquake before I did since she was flat in bed, then I felt it a few seconds later rolling in waves across the floor. I went and stood in the doorway and the door closed on my fingers then opened again. I smelled smoke and thought the building was on fire. Since I was on the sixth floor I thought I was going to die, but it was only the emergency generator coming on. We had a good view of the Marina from the sixth floor and watched it burn. We had TV thanks to the emergency generator, and all of us nurses crowded into one patients room to watch it. My shift ended at midnight and I had to go home in the pitch dark to the mission district that was being looted. When I got home I called my father in England. It was only about 8 AM there, but he had already had many calls from people wanting to know if his daughter was OK."

Through the years, different ideas arose as to what was the safest thing to do during an earthquake. Some people maintain that one should stand in a doorway since it is the strangest part of a building, while others argue it is best to crawl under a large piece of furniture. Of course, it's easy to speculate and debate what to do when an earthquake is not occurring. One man remembered just doing what came naturally: "I was in Redwood City with my dad and we were getting ready to watch the game. He had a small business on El Camino. Things started to shake and he said 'oh, earthquake' but then it REALLY began to shake and I remember this roar as it accelerated in strength. Then he yelled at me to get out. I know you aren't supposed to do that but it is one of the few times I can recall just acting on instinct. Got outside and you could see the street waving and the signal lights were like rubber bands. People in their cars rocking back and forth and a few yelling that Clark just hit one out of the park."

One of the most frightening places to be during the quake was in one of San Francisco's high rise buildings. Fortunately, the newer ones had been designed to withstand powerful earthquakes without collapsing, but there were no guarantees, and anyone inside a high rise was understandably anxious to get out. One woman recounted what that was like: "I was in the Alcoa Building, 20th floor, on the phone w someone local. We both paused then said we're having an earthquake, then hung up. Looked out to see things moving like the street, and an Irish bar below looked like it collapsed down in the street but it was just the facade. Everyone was eerily calm and even joking as we all took stairs to ground level. We didn't know what to do so a coworker and I walked to the water where loudspeakers or something were saying, 'Consult the front pages of the phonebook' re: what to do in this emergency. That still makes me shudder."

Picture of a building façade that has collapsed onto a car

Chapter 3: Pitching In and Helping Out

One worker was killed when a section of St. Joseph's Seminary collapsed in Santa Clara

"Dispatcher: 911 Emergency.

Caller: Is it over yet? 'Cause it don't seem like I can't take much more.

Dispatcher: Ma'am, I know...just hang in there. It's...it's...we hope the worst part is over. The lights are out, the power's out, just hang tight, okay? And it's Ma'am...just hang in there, okay?

Everybody else is scared, too, but we can't...we just don't have the time to stay on the line. So, do this, just make sure your lights are out and if you know where to turn off the gas in your house go turn that off, okay? Make sure you have some fresh water for yourself, okay?

Caller: Okay.

Dispatcher: Okay, so hang in there. It's going to be all right. All right?" - Transcript from a 911 call after the earthquake

Given that native Californians often consider the occasional earthquake to be a natural part of life, many people did not initially realize how bad the earthquake actually was. One native explained, "I was at work at in Fremont. When the quake hit I … got on phone to my wife at home and surprisingly got through. Our home was ½ mile from Loma Prieta Ave in the Santa Cruz Mountains. 'Wow, did you feel that at the house?' I asked casually. Angered at my relaxed attitude, she said hysterically 'the house is destroyed!!' 'Calm down, you're exaggerating. Now, what really happened?' I asked. 'David's (our 18 year old son) car is destroyed, here's David' He got on the phone. 'Dad, the chimney fell off and crushed my new car (just bought it 2 days ago) and the house is destroyed! We're leaving!' … David was upstairs in his room and was thrown to the floor and a large dresser fell on top of him. Desperate to get to his mom downstairs in the kitchen, he threw it off but was thrown down several times. She braced herself between the island and the counter and watched as everything shot out of the cabinets, not just fell. She was struck by dishes, glass, cans, etc. She watched as the 100 ft redwood trees just off our deck swayed at ridiculous angles, smashed into each other, and many large branches broke off and crashed into the house. The sounds were terrifying."

One young woman thought it was safe to return to her apartment and hoped to find that it was still at least somewhat intact. However, she was barely in the building before she realized that there was nothing in there worth risking her life for: "I was living in the South of Market area, on Shipley Street. All the building was tilting at crazy angles, and my apartment building was knocked off its foundations. I managed to get in, though, and nothing was damaged, amazingly. But I smelled gas, so I got out, fearing an explosion. I had one day to remove my belongings, and like thousands of other people, I was temporarily homeless. It was very stressful and depressing, and I eventually had to take a leave of absence from my job just to get my life back in order. Those were really some of the darkest days of my life. Thank god for FEMA; they couldn't find me a new place to live, but they paid for my moving expenses and gave me the money I needed for deposits on a new apartment."

Pictures of collapsed buildings in the Marina district

For parents, the most terrifying thing about the earthquake was the physical and psychological danger it posed to their children. One woman described her experience: "I was at home in San Mateo with my two kids, then 3 and 5. Cupboard doors flew open throwing all the glassware out to the floor, hot water heater cracked in half, it threw full file cabinet drawers open and the files actually were projected out of the drawers all over the floors, power was out for hours afterward. Took quite some time to get everything back in 'order' again. My daughter was so traumatized she completely stopped speaking for four or five hours. Prior to Loma Prieta I used to think earthquakes were fun. The Loma Prieta earthquake changed my line of thinking in that regard forever! I do remember clearly how the next day everyone was still rather shell-shocked and people were much nicer to each other that day - probably the sense of having been through something so traumatic together drew us all a little closer together."

Even in the midst of death and destruction, some people still had the ability to find humor in its situation. Maria Caracol was a newlywed starting to make a fancy dinner for her new husband when the quake hit, and she and her family came up with a unique way to keep in touch in the days that followed: "I live in Sonoma. I had just turned on my dad's wedding gift, a food processor, to make pesto when the house began to tremble. I gawped at the food processor and thought, 'Wow, that's one hell of a machine!'--until I looked out the window and saw the telephone poles across the street waving like palm trees in a storm. My husband was stuck at work in Petaluma. We couldn't call each other and we, our relatives in Davis and our relatives in Emeryville couldn't call each other, but we could all call out of state, so we used a Norwegian grandma in rural Minnesota as our message relay. She just kept clucking her tongue and saying, 'Land sakes!' Even as a native Californian and veteran of earthquakes, it was pretty terrifying. I couldn't believe the extent of the devastation. Truly horrible."

Crises bring out both the best and worst in people, and as night began to fall, the threat of looting soon developed across the city. On the other hand, one woman later recalled how families and friends stuck together to survive the event: ""Electricity was off. Gas was off. Found a radio with batteries. 'The Bay Bridge has collapsed!' they kept repeating. Radio... so of course, all we can make of it is the entire bridge has fallen into the bay. ... We walked over to my parents' house in the Cole Valley (we were on Masonic and Fulton near USF) who were out of town. On the way we saw many buildings with piles of bricks off the walls onto the sidewalks. Many people sat on their steps and talked, it was warm, like I said, and no one had electricity. Clearly nothing was going to happen any time soon, so everyone just talked and got to know the neighbors. At Oak and Masonic some homeless guys were doing traffic control because the streetlights were out. When we got to my parents' house everything on the east side of the house was on the floor (there was no North-South shaking it seemed). Their cinder block bookshelf was in a pile, and the TV and its massive tube was face down on the floor.... We had electricity three days later, and gas about a week after that. I don't remember water ever being a problem."

Of course, the primary concern on most people's minds were finding their families and making sure they were safe. The numbers of those injured by the quake would ultimately approach

4,000, with a total of 63 losing their lives to their injuries, but as the news first trickled in, word spread that there were a number of people trapped in their homes and other buildings. One man relayed a story about how his wife and son were caught in an amazing drama: "My wife and son left the house immediately after we talked but she didn't get very far. A land slide blocked the road. As they sat there wondering what to do, a neighbor woman from the house next to ours came out on the road with her two small children. She was covered with blood. The young children were terrified and crying. Apparently the quake shattered an older plate glass window and cut her badly. Dee and my son got her into the car and bound up her wounds as best they could. Just then another neighbor was trying to get to his house but was blocked by the slide from the other side. After a quick exchange, he climbed over and carried the injured woman and children to his car so he could get her medical help… He was a ranking officer in the Hell's Angels and was doing what real angels do."

With the road out of their neighborhood blocked, the man's family faced a very difficult decision: shelter in place in a badly damaged home or try to go forward on foot. But at that point, another neighbor came to their rescue: "Dee and David were wondering if they should crawl over the slide when another neighbor came around the bend in his bulldozer. He had heard of the slides and fired up his CAT and cleared the slide in about 10 minutes and went on to clear many more into the night. A fireman told them to go to the Middle School on Summit Road as a Red Cross Unit was being set up there and they couldn't get to Santa Cruz or Los Gatos anyway. On arriving the scene was like a Hollywood disaster movie. There were hundreds of people all either evacuated their burnt or collapsed home or prevented getting home due to slides and fallen trees. A Medivac helicopter was departing with the neighbor. She did not look good and had lost a lot of blood. Another neighbor on our road was rescued after her house collapsed on her. Some men with chain saws freed her but her back was broken."

Chapter 4: Protection

Picture of a search and rescue team near a damaged building

"[This call was received on the direct line from the Highway Patrol office at 8th and Harrison Streets, one block from the Hall of Justice.]

California Highway Patrol: We're losing 280. We need all the ramps to 280 closed, if you've got any available units close the traffic coming on to 280 extension up by Sixth Street. It's going down.

Dispatcher: What's going down? The ramp is?

California Highway Patrol: The ramp is. It's collapsing!

Dispatcher: Okay, hold on, I'll tell 'em right now.

California Highway Patrol: Thank you." - Transcript from a 911 call after the earthquake

As soon as the quake stopped shaking the ground, the Langdon's, whose parade in Candlestick had just been preempted, joined their fellow soldiers in making the tricky and arduous journey back to the Presidio. Diane observed, "People were really nice. At the traffic lights nobody was hogging, people weren't panicking, people were actually doing four way stops, and yielding to each other." This was fortunate, since it helped to make a dangerous journey a bit less harrowing. SFC Pellegato, who was with the Langdon's at Candlestick, commented, "Traffic lights were out all over the city but there were civilians on the road that took it upon themselves to go out and help direct traffic. I was amazed at the fact that people really pulled together and took charge." David likewise noted, "Everyone was courteous, we didn't believe how courteous the drivers were, you need to experience it. Civilians were out directing traffic at their own liberty. There were a few negative things but everyone was real cooperative."

From the Presidio, the Langdon's and the others were dispatched all over the city to help where needed. David was sent to the Marina District, one of the hardest hit sections of San Francisco: "I had assumed the position of Patrol Supervisor of the Day Shift here at the Presidio. I was in charge of a normal five man patrol that was extended to twelve hour shifts (rather than the normal eight hours), plus doing shuttle runs from the Presidio and Command Post out to the Command Post set up down at Divisadero in the Marina District. I don't know if you would call it fortunate or unfortunate, to see the destruction wrought by the fires and quake down in the Marina District. ... I couldn't even tell you how many trips I made with elderly that couldn't walk, some of them were in wheelchairs. We just placed them in the [patrol] cars and took them outside the perimeter of the damaged area. The shock of the people that had lost everything was terrible to witness."

Picture of a journalist preparing to report from the Marina district

Meanwhile, things at Vincent Milano's fire station were not so calm. They knew that they were moments away from being called upon to help in the crisis, but they were concerned about how they would find out who needed help because so many of the devices they depended on for information were out of commission. Milano explained, "When the earthquake hit, right afterwards, our computer veg'd out. It was basically gone. The computer controls all water-flow alarms, some manual pull-box alarms, smoke detectors, especially at Letterman Army Institute of Research and Letterman Army Medical Center (LAMC) and Fort Baker, Berry and Cronkite [in the Marin Headlands]. Our telephone lines were on, the emergency line was working, our radios were working. Except we had a major problem of 'bleed-over' from the MP's and everybody else."

In addition to the loss of power and water, many people faced a transportation crisis. Elizabeth Stelow was working on the 16th floor of a newly built office building when the earthquake hit, and though she and the others in the building were uninjured, new construction regulations left them with other problems. She explained, "Perhaps my biggest challenge related to the earthquake was my inability to get my car. The parking garage in the Financial District where I parked used elevators to move cars from the entrance to the actual parking floors. My car was on the third floor and the lack of electricity prevented me from getting it out. If I had been living in San Francisco at the time, this would not have been such a problem. But my apartment was in Foster City, some 15 miles south. Fortunately my boyfriend (now husband) had just given me a key to his apartment on Clay Street. So, I grabbed a change of clothes from my car, as well as a nice young lady I met in the parking garage, and headed for his apartment. The reason I took pity on the other stranded driver (Judy), was that she had driven up to San Francisco from San Mateo for a job interview that started at 5:00 (and, it would seem, ended promptly at 5:03). As amusing as I found her story, I felt terrible that she had no place else to go."

As was traditionally the case during the last half of the 20th century, a government head was soon sent to California to survey the damage, and David Langdon got to witness this firsthand: "I had to escort a few of the military dignitaries so they could survey the situation to insure that the military was actually needed. While I was down there on one occasion, dropping supplies off to our MPs, radios and food, I happened to get caught up the arrival of Vice-President Quayle and his entourage. I had absolutely no chance to get out of the area. I was immediately summoned by the Secret Service detail for the performance of security and holding back the press and any onlookers from the Vice-President, so he could have an unimpeded passage through the Marina District to view the destruction. That was an experience, just couldn't stay far enough away to where the Secret Service [was happy]."

A severely damaged entryway in the Marina district

While the Vice President of the United States had a good reason to be at the scene and was welcomed by most of those there, other visitors flocking to the area only exacerbated matters instead of improving them. David later remembered, "And then what was really worse were the onlookers. The tourists that would come in and gape and stare at someone else's disadvantaged position for their own benefit. We couldn't do much better than keeping them as far back as we could and just try to help the civilian populace as much as possible. You couldn't do any more for them, all their possessions were gone, what they had was what was on their backs. Those that were fortunate could get back into their living areas for a short period of time. After the third day I did not go down there as much as I should have, the pressure was just too much. It was ... it was enough. I had to try and maintain myself here and maintain a patrol and the security of Presidio."

Naturally, as light began to fade that night, the city and its citizens became much harder to protect. People could get around in daylight, but power was out over most of the city, so the streetlights and traffic lights that many depended on to get from one place to another were out of order. Michael Bello, the student who had been stuck in the elevator, recalled, "As the darkness hit the city…the intersections were just stopped, no traffic lights…pure darkness! I had instructed an uncle to take the freeway to pick me up in South of Market at 3rd and Folsom! BIG MISTAKE! No Cellphones at the time and land lines were dead. It took him 2 hours to get to where I am and another 3 hours to get to the Sunset District of San Francisco at 38th Avenue and Lincoln. I made it home right before midnight…to find out that everything was off the walls and the whole place was strewn with debris…"

All the while, firefighters and law enforcement had to continue helping others before they could worry about themselves, even as the work meant they were risking their own lives. One man witnessed firsthand some of the ways the earthquake affected those dedicated to public service: "We went into town looking for a pay phone that might work. I was amazed at the broken concrete sidewalks and shattered storefronts. Yuppie couples were strolling along the broken streets taking in the scene sipping from wine glasses they carried. A pay phone was found working at the Bakers Square Restaurant. I watched as an obviously exhausted police officer using the phone to call his family. I could hear him telling them that he was OK and asking who had been heard from. He instructed them to turn off gas valves and such and stay put. He would be on duty indefinitely and try to talk to them later. It struck me what true dedication costs these public heroes in disasters."

Chapter 5: The Fires

"[Man on phone has reported minor broken window and requested the Fire Department.]

Dispatcher: Sir! Listen to me.

Caller: Yeah?

Dispatcher: The whole city is experiencing an emergency crisis at this time. If nobody's hurt find some way to barricade this window on your own. In the meantime, the whole city is going chaotic right now, okay?

Caller: All right.

Dispatcher: Okay, thank you… .

Caller: The Fire Department isn't available?

Dispatcher: The Fire Department is busy answering fires. They're doing everything they can right now.

Caller: Are there any fires?

Dispatcher: Yes there was fires. Sir, I have to hang up the line now, okay?

Caller: All right.

Dispatcher: Thank you." - Transcript from a 911 call after the earthquake

One thing residents of the Bay Area knew all too well is that earthquakes are almost always followed by fires. The fires that spread after the 1906 earthquake destroyed gas lines and water lines were so devastating that San Franciscans typically referred to the disaster as "the Fire." While modern technology has mitigated that problem to a certain extent, and the Bay Area even took extra lengths to ensure access to water in the event of an earthquake causing fires, there is only so much that can be done, and within minutes of 1989 earthquake, the flames were burning across the city. Firefighter Vincent Milano remembered, "At 5:59, we received a call from San Francisco Fire Department Chief. ... I answered the phone and the communications officer on the line reported a fire at Beach and Divisadero. He wanted to know if we could respond mutually on the call. I told him hold on a minute. Captain Smith was standing right next to me, I told him what we had, he took a second to think about it because, he can't arbitrarily just send us out on a mutual-aid call, he's got procedures to follow. ... He made the decision to send Engine 2, which was the only apparatus in the Station at the time. Engine 1 was at LAMC, Rescue 1 was at the water, and 82 was out with Rescue 1. So he made the decision to send myself and Roy Evans, he's the driver/operator. ... We have two portables [radios] for the City that we can talk to them on, so we grabbed one of those and one of our [Presidio] portable radios. We didn't know at the time that the city radio was down. So, we didn't try to contact them anyway. We just kept in contact with our station."

Milano would later note how grateful he was to have Evans with him that day, saying, "Consider him a veteran, he's been with the California Department of Forestry, he's been through a great deal fire-wise, so it's good to have him because he tried to keep me down to earth. I mean, [I'm a] rookie, not knowing what's going on it's kind of hard to keep control."

Nevertheless, the "rookie" was about to join the big leagues. Milano continued, "Between that time we left, and we got out the gate, our sirens running and the horn yelling [this] is kinda the fun part of the job. Then we smelled the smoke and it was like a different feeling. I don't know how to explain it. It was like 'this is for real.' I've had grass fires here in the Presidio and at Fort Baker and all, but I never expected to actually go to a fire. So, we were going down Marina Boulevard to Divisadero and there were people out along the streets were waving their hands and telling which streets to go down. We knew where we going, but seeing them going like that, well this has got to be the street to go down. You could see the smoke from a long way off. People across the Bay could see the smoke. When we made the right hand turn on Divisadero, I can't remember what we said, but we basically both said, s–, because there it was, when we saw what we were getting into."

A picture of the damage at the intersection of Beach and Divisadero

The fire proved to be much worse than either man had anticipated. The long, hot California summer had been drier than usual, and the city's homes, especially its older ones, were powder kegs waiting to explode. By opening up gas lines and knocking cooking pans off of stoves, the earthquake provided a giant match to set explosions off, and Milano had the unfortunate experience of witnessing the conflagration: "It was about two blocks away, we were coming in, there were people on the site helping everybody. As we just pull up to it, we are about three houses away from it. Roy, I guess through his experience seeing death and all, was very cool, he was telling me what needed to be done. I was a space cadet, I heard him, but I wasn't sure that I was going to do exactly what he said. I wasn't sure until I started doing stuff. It turned out to be all right, we both did what we were supposed to do. But I was still up there ... I couldn't bring myself down, it was a different feeling. You were able to do your job, but it was still feeling ... things were just going through your mind so fast.... We reported to the Station [Presidio] that we were on scene, reported what we had, and we both got out of the engine. Roy was sizing up the situation; San Francisco Police Officers came up to me and said there was a woman trapped next door, not directly next door to the building that was on fire because that one had collapsed."

A picture of smoldering rubble at Beach and Divisadero

An aerial view of damaged and leaning buildings at Beach and Divisadero in the Marina district

At this point, Milano's training kicked in, and he was able to render the assistance he was asked to provide. However, with just two men fighting a large burning building, they quickly had to prioritize what their first move would be. As always, the first goal was to save those in danger. As Milano recalled, "We grabbed axes, there's one on each side where the hoseman usually sits, and we went up there and I broke the door window for the cop to get access. He said he could get her out. I went down and hooked up back with Roy. We laid our two and half inch line, which is the biggest line we have, just to the right of the fire. Roy started pumping the water. By that time, we were the first engine on the scene. By the time we got our hose hooked up and started pumping water, the City had gotten there and they supplied us with lines into our Engine, and started pumping water.... They hooked up to the hydrant which was working for 20 minutes after the earthquake. The aftershocks knocked them out. ... After that died down, we went off the tank water we had left in our [engine]."

From the very beginning, it was an uphill battle for the men working to contain the fires, let alone extinguish them; not only were there more blazes than the combined departments could cope with, there was also a water shortage caused by a combination of broken water pipes and high demand. Milano noted, "We got on the scene at 1821 hours (6:21 PM), we pumped water for approximately 15-20 minutes off a hydrant, then Roy did his engineering techniques on the Engine to make the water in the Engine last for approximately another 5-10 minutes. We basically had water going on the building for a half hour. [When] we ran out of water, the fire just kept escalating. It caught the building where that woman was trapped on fire. The building that was initially on fire started collapsing. After we ran out of water, it did catch on fire, the radiation or heat was so intense. It just toasted it."

It soon became clear that the house they were originally sent to save was a lost cause. At that point, according to Milano, "We were doing exposure, meaning we were trying to save the house to the right and was fire-free from catching. I don't know if it did any good because it just looked like we were shooting the water onto the side of it and it looked like it was just turning to steam."

At this point, he realized that what he was dealing with went far beyond any fire he had ever worked before: "The fire just kept building and the heat was...Well you didn't want your turn-out coat on or anything because you just boiled inside. It was real hot. Our faces were the only things that got exposed, and we got like a mild sunburn or heat burn. We were kind of red afterwards. You didn't notice it at the time, your adrenaline is just going. Mine was anyway, I don't know about anyone else. ... The air was very dry and still. There was no wind, so everything was going straight up in the air. The heat basically dried out your lungs, but as long as you were going, you didn't notice any of this stuff until later."

There were also problems with communication, as Milano also pointed out: "But during the time I was holding the hose, not one City firefighter helped out. I had civilians in shorts, short-sleeved shirts, no shirts, they were behind me holding the hose. Roy and I had to pick up the hose and back up the Engine three times the heat was so bad. The first two times we pulled back 30 feet or so. I think the third time after we got all the hose loaded we could, we backed it clear out of there and took [the Engine] around the block. [We] didn't need to be in anymore and we didn't have any water. ... After the building that was burning [collapsed]. The smoke got real bad because [the fire] was basically smothering and burning itself out. But the building on the right side was starting to go, so until the [SFFD Fireboat] Phoenix got their tie line and everything in.... At that point the San Francisco Fire Department took over and the Presidio Fire Department returned to the Station. While Engine 2 of the Presidio Fire Department was fighting the Marina fire casualties from the Bay Bridge were brought to the helipad at Crissy Field."

According to Edward J. Phipps, a former chief of the San Francisco Fire Department, the toll taken by fire was not nearly as serious as it might otherwise have been, thanks in large part to the assistance the Fire Department received from volunteers. He wrote, "There were several fires, of which six were classified as major. There were also natural gas leaks, broken water pipes, explosions and emergency medical calls. The EMS system was quickly overwhelmed, and members of the Fire Prevention Bureau were given first aid kits and then assigned to assist the County Ambulance Service which handled medical calls. This had the effect of allowing the department's street apparatus to handle other emergencies."

Chapter 6: The Bay Bridge

A picture of a collapsed section of the Bay Bridge

"Dispatcher: 911 Emergency.

Caller: Yes, have you gotten word about the Bay Bridge?

Dispatcher: What about the Bay Bridge? What's wrong with it?

Caller: The upper deck appears to have collapsed during the earthquake.

Dispatcher: "S–t! Hold on a second! Jesus Christ! We gotta report that right away! That might have collapsed on the CALIFORNIA HIGHWAY PATROL!" - Transcript from a 911 call after the earthquake

One of the most traumatic losses for the city of San Francisco that day was the beloved Bay Bridge. Although the small number of casualties incurred by the collapse of a section of the bridge was incredibly fortuitous, those who had the misfortune of being on any part of the bridge that day had an experience they never forgot. One driver later wrote, "I was driving westbound on the Bay Bridge in 1989 hoping I'd get home before I missed much of the Giants/A's World Series Game Three on the TV. I was on the upper deck, but was luckily past the part that collapsed. I had just emerged from the Treasure Island tunnel. It felt first like my car was having a flat tire and then I realized, no, it was the bridge swaying like a hammock. And I thought, this could be the end, but that seemed OK --- like whatever would happen was part of some plan. All the cars slowly came to a halt as if on cue. It was totally quiet except for the creaking of the bridge as it stretched its limits; eerie, yet peaceful. And when the swaying stopped, all the cars began, again as if on cue, driving hesitantly forward to see what havoc nature had wrought in San Francisco."

Kurt Mercier was sent to help move victims being flown in from the bridge to nearby hospitals, and he expected the worst: "I jumped in the patrol car with SGT Tabor and SGT Shephard. We got down to the helipad and while we were there all we could think about was how sad we were, we couldn't believe the Bay Bridge had collapsed. We pictured several hundred casualties coming in, knowing that [traffic] at that time of day was bad."

Fortunately, the World Series had compelled many people to leave work early, either to attend the game or watch it, so the traffic was lighter than normal that day. Still, there were many injured people needing help, including Anamafi Moala and her brother Lesisita Halangahu. After the shaking stopped, she failed to see a hole left by the collapse of the bridge and drove into it. The two were extracted from their car and taken to the helipad, where Mercier picked them up: "The Coast Guard chopper came down and one of the chopper personnel ran toward us. He said that the girl didn't look like she was in good shape, possibly she was dead. They also had a second casualty, a male, who was in pretty bad shape. We could see he had bleeding from the chest, compound fractures in both legs, he had his arms crossed over his chest and was in a semi-conscious state. I was trying to tell the guy just from experience that if he was going into shock, just try to prevent it, he was going to be okay, he was going to be all right…. I could see he'd look up at me and I...kept repeating that to give him some type of hope. So we calmed him down, he gives a little nod like he understood, I was just holding on to him...holding his hand with mine...reassuring him. I heard the doctor behind me saying, 'Somebody start CPR.' I turned around, one medic was standing over, about two feet away just looking down at her like he was pretty shocked...maybe he hadn't seen this before. I released the hand of the guy and turned around and started doing chest compressions on her. It was pretty difficult at first since her ribs were through her chest cavity and they started to cut my hands. The doctor saw that and he gave me a cervical collar (neck brace). I put it over her chest to keep [her broken ribs] from penetrating my skin."

Anamafi had lost a lot of blood and was still bleeding, but no one was ready to give up. Mercier continued, "We were trying to load her into the ambulance…I grabbed one side while doing chest compressions with one hand and grabbing the gurney [with] the other, the doctor had her head, while SGT Taber grabbed the other side and we put her in the ambulance. We sat in the ambulance, continued compression and continued with the air. Once en route…the doctor had to stop doing CPR because she had a pulse. That lasted four or five beats, then it stopped again so he said continue. I continued CPR as we unloaded her and all the way into the Emergency Room at which time I was relieved by a doctor. I was still in sweats and I wasn't wearing my brassard that says you're on duty or anything. But I still knew I had the duty to go back out." Tragically, Mercier later learned that the woman, Anamafi Moala, 23 years old and married for exactly one month to the day, was pronounced dead on arrival at the hospital.

Thankfully, Anamafi was the only fatality caused by the collapsed section of the Bay Bridge, so Mercier spent that rest of his duty during the crisis attached to the San Francisco Police Department. He described what he saw back in the city: "There were a lot of people still walking around in tears and a few people hurt … with cuts and bruises … Just everyone dazed, just confused, not knowing what to do, where to go, firefighters and San Francisco Police Department all over. It's hard to tell someone that they can't go back in their home. It may not be easy for them to see safety-wise but that was our main concern. We didn't have to tussle with anyone we just talked to them, and tried to explain. Here again these people were confused, angry, frustrated, and everything else combined so they were like a firecracker getting ready to go off. We just had to talk calmly to them and explain to them the reasons why they couldn't go back in. Here again trying to give them the reassurance that everything would be okay, you know it's bad, but you're okay, you're physically okay, you're doing all right, that was the main factor for them."

Some of the health professionals found themselves on duty even though they were thousands of miles from home. One of them, Mary Belle Scott, was on vacation in San Francisco when the quake hit, and at that moment, she realized her vacation came to an abrupt end: "My husband and I…were on the Bay Bridge heading to Oakland. Suddenly we ran over something, or so I thought. The radio deejay announced 'Whoa, that was a big one.' I was still looking for what we had run over when John told us that we had just experienced our first earthquake. He pulled off at the next exit and we came to a stop. I was an ER nurse so I got out hoping I could help in some way. I walked around a broad curve to the right and there was an awesome awful sight. The upper tier of the freeway was buckled and collapsed for as far as I could see. I was amazed that the fire department was already there, hard at work. I climbed a fire ladder to the upper deck, with many people helping to steady the ladder. … This is the strongest memory I have of that day - the people who wanted to help as they could. I was able to give a little help to a woman named Trish. ... My only scary time was when a helicopter seemed about to land some distance away. At the same time the upper deck began vibrating and shaking again. I don't know if this was downwash from the helicopter or an aftershock but the helicopter took off without landing. I was afraid right then! But I decided to stick with Trish and things settled down shortly."

Although the Bay Bridge mostly stayed intact, the age of the bridge led city officials to decide to rebuild the eastern span of the bridge instead of just strengthening the old one. Furthermore, despite the uncertainty over when another big earthquake will strike, city politicians still dragged their feet over certain characteristics of the reconstruction project, including picking a design. The eastern span was originally planned to be done in 2004, but it remains unfinished. One team of researchers suggested in 1992 that the eastern span should be retrofitted instead of replaced, which would have cost under $250 million, but instead, the newly rebuilt span is expected to open in 2016 and cost over $7 billion.

Oleg Alexandrov's 2013 picture of the revamped Bay Bridge, which is still undergoing construction

Chapter 7: Surviving the Aftermath

"Dispatcher: 911 Emergency.

Caller: My whole house is tore up! Should I take my kids outside?

Dispatcher: Your whole house what?

Caller: It's tore up! Everything's tore up, should I take my kids outside?

Dispatcher: Yeah, that would be a good idea because here comes another one!"

San Francisco is known for its hills, but while people might normally enjoy climbing them in comfortable shoes, many people found themselves walking in all the wrong places in all the wrong shoes after the earthquake. One man, Chris Cory, left his office planning to make his way home on foot, but he described just how difficult that turned out to be:

> "The entire downtown scene was chaos. The traffic lights were out, and none of the electric transportation was working. Traffic was snarled in a stagnation of uncoordinated signals. People milled around as if lost in a drugged stupor. The experienced darted to catch ferries which took them out of town. The bars were dark, but lit with candles, and full of people who were talking wildly over the day's event and drinking tapped beer. The doors were flung open, and people spilled out onto the street. The sense of community was palpable.
>
> I began walking home, because none of the trains were working. I had just purchased a cheap set of Hungarian dress shoes which I wore all the way through the soles that day. After half an hour of walking, I decided to grab a MUNI (the San Francisco transportation system.) After riding it for several blocks, I decided that it was moving no faster than I was, so I got out and walked the rest of the way."

For others, the aftermath of the earthquake would prove to be more terrifying than the quake itself. The man who initially thought his wife was exaggerating when told their house and their son's car had been destroyed found himself desperate to get to his wife and family at a nearby friend's house. He remembered, "They were going to a friend's house in Santa Cruz and I would meet them there. We were unaware we would go through 15 hours of hell until we met. The phones were useless from that point. I got in my car and started home from Fremont. I usually listen to KGO for breaking Bay Area News, but no signal. On driving by their transmission towers near Dumbarton Bridge I saw why, their towers were down. I got to Los Gatos without much incident but found Hwy 17 into the Santa Cruz Mountains and home was closed. The CALIFORNIA HIGHWAY PATROL said road was buckled and impassable and no telling how long before it opened. I went to a bar in downtown Los Gatos that was open with a lot of people arriving telling what they knew. Los Gatos had power and TV was working. A group invited me and some fellow stranded Hwy 17 commuters to their house in town for food and possible phone use. About 20 of us congregated at this house and watched for news on TV."

Picture of a collapsed section of Pacific Garden Mall in Santa Cruz

The way in which families were separated from each other and unable to get in touch only heightened the sense of despair and panic. By 1989, most people in the United States were used to being able to pick up a telephone and call someone whenever they wanted to, whereas the victims of past earthquakes knew it would be hours or days before they knew what was going on. Those who lived through the 1989 earthquake were accustomed to having access to news in minutes, and when people realized they were out of the loop, many panicked. The man who desperately tried to get to his wife and son observed this for himself: "Occasionally, one of us would go check out the roadblock on Hwy 17 for status. Many of these stranded commuters had families up in the Santa Cruz Mountains they were unable to reach. From Los Gatos, we could see plumes up in the mountains and realized these were fires caused by propane tanks breaking loose from their mounts. Several moms were hysterical since they had kids at home up there and no way to get to them, talk to them, or know if they were ok. By now we learned the epicenter was in the SC Mountains (the very hills we were looking at) and it measured a 7.1 Richter. I felt so fortunate that I had talked to my wife and son if even briefly and could only imagine what these others felt who had no communication with their families at home. We watched TV reports of the Bay Bridge and collapsed Apartment houses in the Marina in SF and wondered what the destruction was like in the mountains on the epicenter. It was frustrating as there was no news coverage anywhere near the epicenter in Santa Cruz County since like us, the crews couldn't get there."

Even in places where there was more information available, people had a difficult time coping with what had happened. Rick Ferry was at home when the quake hit and suffered only minor damage to his residence. In that sense, he was one of the lucky ones, but he was still left in shock by what he was seeing: "The telephone system was briefly overwhelmed but the power was still on. The television station continued to broadcast. There were pictures of the Watsonville and Santa Cruz areas (failed brick structures mostly). Unfiltered pictures were shown of the dead being pulled out of debris (mostly brick walls and facades). Raw footage of the Cypress Freeway showed smoke and dust. The commenter had no idea initially that the freeway had collapsed and the injured, dead and dying where trapped underneath. Later, there were pictures of brave souls who climbed the structures using ladders, climbing over debris trying to help people who were trapped. The aftershocks came. The help continued."

Pictures of the collapsed Cypress Street Viaduct, which killed 40 people in Oakland

Of course, there are always some people in life who, no matter what the circumstances they find themselves in, manage to land on their feet. Bob Beecher, a single man from out of town, found a way to make the best of a bad situation: "On the ill-fated day, I flew up to San Jose Airport to spend the day observing and training our new agents, mostly young women. At the end of the day, I remember standing on the reservations floor...and then the building shook. My native California experience led me to shout, "Get under your desks!" as I dove underneath an empty desk nearby. Surprisingly, another young lady saw the same desk and wedged herself into the already cramped space next to me and then dug her fingernails into my left forearm as she tensed. 'Aaaaagh!' ... After about a half-hour, Nancy, the office manager, upon hearing some of the early damage reports on the radio, told the young ladies that those who lived nearby could go home; but those who lived in the outlying areas should probably not be on the road. Most traffic signals were out and debris and rockslides were a hazard to those driving in the hills. I was also stranded due to the airport.... The manager gave the seven or eight stranded ladies her home address in Mountain View and told them they were going to bunk there tonight. The best part? I got to sleep over as well! YES!! We all had a very nice party that night!"

On October 21, four days after the disaster, the situation was secure enough to allow President Bush to visit the area. Again, David Langdon was involved in crowd control: "I spent numerous hours with Operations here setting up for his arrival with the San Francisco Police and Secret

Service. He landed, all things went well. My wife was part of the human barricade right at the aircraft, the reporters knocked her literally within three feet of the President. He (President Bush) met with Mayor Art Agnos. Of course, he had his entourage of Senators and press, and he flew out to survey the destruction of the Cypress structure [in Oakland] and [the city] of Watsonville. Things went very smoothly for us. On the fifth day following the earthquake there was a recall back to our own areas of operation here at the Presidio. The San Francisco Police and California Highway Patrol appreciated our services. Mayor Agnos appreciated us for reacting as quickly as we did. Recognition ceremonies were held on post and Presidio soldiers and civilian heroes marched in the 1990 Armed Forces Day Parade. Among the valiant were Firefighter Vince Milano and Roy Evans with Engine 2."

A picture of President Bush surveying the damage suffered by the Cypress Street Viaduct

As is always the case following a catastrophe, many people turned to their faith and sought to find the good in what had happened. Church attendance improved temporarily as people sought both solace and shelter. Likewise, people turned to each other, asking why such things happen and looking for answers from both inside themselves and the opinions of those around them. Murray McCool found both spiritual and financial comfort following the earthquake, as he later related: "The rest of the evening (of October 17) was spent watching the reports pouring in from all around the Bay. We had the meeting at our home as scheduled, but by 7:30 our power had gone out and we had to light up a lantern while a group of about 20 gathered to study the Bible. We all noted how earthquakes would be one mark of what Jesus Christ called the 'last days'. Ten days later, the City of Oakland hired me as a Building Inspector. The first two months of my employment included damage assessment of structures and homes, and escorting visiting volunteer structural engineers around town to observe the damage first hand, scooting back and forth under what was left of the destroyed Cypress Freeway. It was the best experience a novice building inspector could ever gain."

As Murray McCool's account indicated, just like in 1906, plans to revitalize and improve the Bay Area were underway just as quickly as the damage had been done.

Bibliography

Fradkin, Philip L. (1999) *Magnitude 8: Earthquakes and Life Along the San Andreas Fault*, University of California Press.

Gunn, Angus M. (2007) *Encyclopedia of Disasters: Environmental Catastrophes and Human Tragedies*, Greenwood Publishing Group.

Housner, G. W. (1990), *Competing Against Time - Report to Governor George Deukmejian from The Governor's Board of Inquiry on the 1989 Loma Prieta Earthquake*, State of California, Office of Planning and Research.

McDonnell, J. A. (1993), *Response to the Loma Prieta Earthquake*, United States Government Printing Office.

Made in the USA
San Bernardino, CA
19 March 2018